The Road

The Canadian Corps 1914-1918

1969
Macmillan of Canada
Toronto

peter zegers

The Road Past Vimy

The Road

The Canadian Corps 1914-1918

1969
Macmillan of Canada
Toronto

Past Vimy

D. J. GOODSPEED

The maps in this book, except that on p. 15, were drawn by Mr. W. R. Bennett, and first appeared in *Battle Royal, A History of the Royal Regiment of Canada* by D. J. Goodspeed, published by the Royal Regiment of Canada Association in 1962. Grateful acknowledgment is made to the Royal Regiment of Canada Association for permission to reproduce them here.

Printed in Canada by The Bryant Press Limited for The Macmillan Company of Canada Limited 70 Bond Street, Toronto

Contents

List of photographs   vii
List of maps   ix
Chapter One   1
Chapter Two   18
Chapter Three   39
Chapter Four   64
Chapter Five   80
Chapter Six   94
Chapter Seven   109
Chapter Eight   124
Chapter Nine   138
Chapter Ten   154
The Canadian Corps in France – major formations and units   175
Sources   177
Index   180

Photographs

(all from the Public Archives of Canada)

(between pages 48 and 49)
Lunch time in the trenches
The cathedral at Ypres
A visit from Sir Sam Hughes
A soldier receiving first aid
No-man's-land, Courcelette
The "Hanging Virgin" at Albert
Canadian troops returning from the trenches
A Canadian soldier
Canadian machine gunners at Vimy Ridge
Firing a captured gun
A tank in action

(between pages 112 and 113)
A Canadian battalion on the march
A Canadian ammunition column

The battlefield at Passchendaele
Germans surrendering at Vimy Ridge
Passchendaele
German and Canadian wounded
Canadian heavy artillerymen
Observation post

(between pages 144 and 145)
Haig and Currie
Troops march past Sir Robert Borden
Canadian troops near Amiens
Captured trenches near Arras
The square at Cambrai
Festubert
Duck's Bill Crater
A crater at St. Eloi
Givenchy

Maps

The Western Front, 1914-1918   15
Ypres, 1915   23
Festubert and Givenchy, May-June 1915   47
Mount Sorrel, June 1916   62
The Somme, September-October 1916   75
Vimy Ridge, April 1917   86
Passchendaele, October-November 1917   116
Amiens, August 1918   144
Drocourt-Quéant Line, September 1918   161
Canal du Nord and Bourlon Wood, September 1918   166

The Road Past Vimy

The summer the old world died was a lovely one in Canada. June had been perfect, if a little dry, with high blue skies and cool nights. July had been hot, but not unbearably so; the harvest was mostly in; and from the Maritimes to the West Coast the country was quiet and serene, with a serenity that was then an accustomed thing but has since been forgotten.

In 1914 there were rather fewer than eight million Canadians – the 1911 census had recorded 7,206,643 – and most of them lived on the farm or in small, sleepy villages that were the recognizable prototypes of Stephen Leacock's Mariposa. The Canadian West was still in some sense a frontier, and the older, more settled regions of the country regarded it with a romantic eye. Ralph Connor's new book, *The Patrol of the Sun Dance Trail*, was selling well in the East that summer, and *The Girl of the Golden West* had just opened in Toronto at the Royal Alexandra Theatre. Suffragettes were agitating for equal rights for women; prohibitionists in Ontario had tried to have the bar-rooms closed; and the hobble skirt had come into fashion.

There was never to be another summer like this one; the war that broke out at the beginning of August would see to that. At the time, and during the years following the Armistice, people called the conflict the Great War. When it broke out again in 1939, the nomenclature was changed and people spoke of the period of fighting between 1914 and 1918 as the

First World War and of that between 1939 and 1945 as the Second World War. In truth, it was all one war, just as the Peloponnesian Wars were all one war.

The immediate pretext for the war, of course, was what happened in Sarajevo on the quiet Sunday morning of June 28, 1914. Young Gabriel Princip, a Bosnian student, stepped out of the crowd that lined the Appel Quay and shot to death the heir apparent to the Austrian throne. The murder had been planned by members of a Serbian secret society, colloquially known as the Black Hand, that desired to create a great South Slav state in the Balkans at the expense of the Austro-Hungarian Empire. Austria, glad of the excuse to chastise a troublesome neighbour, determined to force a war on Serbia. This was bad enough, but what made the situation truly frightening was that Germany was allied to Austria and stood behind her, as the Kaiser had said, "in shining armour". At this time Germany was generally regarded as a bumptious parvenu rather than as an ogre crouched in the centre of Europe, but undoubtedly she was very well prepared for war. German diplomacy, however, had been less adept than German arms, and since 1894 France, who remembered her defeat of 1870 and dreamed of recovering the lost provinces of Alsace and Lorraine, had been allied with Russia in the Dual Entente, threatening Germany on the east and the west.

When Austria sent Serbia a stiff ultimatum on July 23, the German government, although it had not even seen the text of the note, virtually underwrote the Austrian threats. To do him justice, the Kaiser believed that only a little war would result, one in which Austria could defeat Serbia without interference. He was certain that Europe would not support a nation "that had stained itself by assassination".

He was wrong. It has since been confirmed – and in the summer of 1914 there was good reason to believe – that the Serbian cabinet, and possibly certain members of the Serbian royal family, possessed guilty foreknowledge of the Black Hand murder, but Russia, anxious to forestall revolution at home by triumphs abroad, supported her Balkan protégé. France, mindful of her period of isolation after 1870, clung to Russia and did nothing to moderate Russian intransigence over the Austrian-Serbian quarrel.

However, these were no more than the superficial causes of the conflict. There was, in truth, a fatal mood in Europe. It was a worldly, prosperous, arrogant age, and there was a strange restlessness abroad. For decades every major power had proclaimed a vulgar nationalism that was offensive to its rivals and ludicrous to its allies. Armaments had steadily increased, international tensions had continually heightened through a series of crises, and – at least in Russia, Austria-Hungary, and Germany – soldiers had moved nearer to the heart of affairs. In every country some men in high position were half in love with war.

None of this, it would have been thought, concerned Canadians in the least, and it seemed ridiculous to suppose that Nova Scotian fishermen or Manitoban farmers could possibly be touched by anything that happened in some out-of-the-way corner of southeastern Europe. Even after the murder of the Archduke Franz Ferdinand, few Canadians were seriously concerned. They shared only vicariously in the fears and hatreds of Europe; recurrent crises over the past ten years had ended without bloodshed; and war was little more than a word to them. Moreover, times were none too good in Canada; economic problems loomed larger than Balkan quarrels. In 1914 the acreage of field crops was less than in any year since 1910. Canadian industries were working at only one-half to three-quarters of their capacity. And a movement had begun to deport unemployed immigrants to their countries of origin. Prior to June 28, most Canadians would have had the utmost difficulty in locating Sarajevo on the map, and before the actual outbreak of war very few had been heard to suggest that Tsarist Russia was interested in making the world safe for democracy. The Balkans, indeed, were scarcely to be taken seriously, except as settings for exotic adventure novels like *Graustark* or *The Prisoner of Zenda*. The assassination of an archduke by a secret society was only what might be expected in such outlandish places. Canadian newspapers were much more interested in Ulster's opposition to Home Rule or in the scandalous murder trial of Madame Cailleux, a French cabinet minister's wife who had shot the editor of *Le Figaro*.

It is true that the strength of the Canadian Militia had

grown from 36,000 in 1904 to 59,000 in 1914 and that the Minister of Militia, Colonel Sam Hughes, had bullied his cabinet colleagues into increasing the defence budget by three and a half million dollars. "Germany has to be taught a lesson," Hughes had declaimed in Vancouver as early as 1912, and he never tired of repeating this belligerent sentiment. In July 1914 he concentrated more than 10,000 militiamen at Camp Petawawa for summer training. But since Hughes had a habit of self-glorification,* these preparations could as easily have been an expression of his egotism as a reflection of real danger.

Until late in July even the Conservative Prime Minister, Sir Robert Borden, took the view that the crisis would not affect Canada in any way. Sir Robert was the soul of honour and, as Sam Hughes half-contemptuously said, "as gentle-hearted as a girl", but he had been in power less than three years and in 1914 he was unusually willing – even for his party and generation – to follow an imperial lead. For him, as for most English-speaking Canadians, the intricacies of international politics were simplified by a few forthright convictions. The British way was best. One flag, one fleet, one throne. What we have we hold. Borden was sure that Britain was not allied with either European power bloc and that the British Liberal government had no wish to become involved in a European war. In the self-governing colonies the Victorian certainties had survived beyond their time.

What Borden did not know was that in 1905 Sir Edward Grey, the British Foreign Secretary, without informing all his cabinet colleagues, had authorized secret staff conversations between the British and French armies. Thus, although there was no formal commitment, Britain was morally bound to the Dual Entente. The Canadian Prime Minister, remembering the diplomatic exchange that had preceded the South African War, was convinced "that Great Britain would never engage in war without consulting the Dominions", but in

* In 1904, for instance, on the basis of brief and undistinguished service as a transport officer in the rear areas in South Africa, Hughes had declared that he had earned not one but two Victoria Crosses and demanded that the Canadian government see that "justice" was done him. The British War Office ruled that he was not entitled even to the war gratuity.

4

fact, when the crisis came, he was not informed until July 28 that Britain "would almost certainly be involved if France was attacked". Even so, Sir Robert seems to have been told this unpalatable truth before it was communicated to all the British cabinet, many of whom still believed neutrality possible.

In Britain, as in other nations, there were undercurrents of mood that were swept willingly along with the drift to war. Certain influential admirals, generals, and senior Foreign Office officials were anxious for a confrontation with Germany, and British ruling circles in general had long been sensitive to Germany's increasing wealth and power and were uncomfortably aware that Britain's early Victorian industrial supremacy had been waning for decades. Symptomatic of this change in relative position, and more dramatically challenging, was the fact that Germany had begun to build a High Seas Fleet, which in communications, design, armour, and probably gunnery had a ship-to-ship superiority over the Royal Navy.

The emotions these facts aroused in some quarters in Britain were fully shared by the Canadian Prime Minister. As long ago as 1910 Borden had said: "If the Germans prove themselves the greater race, if they have greater resourcefulness, higher skill, superior organizing ability, and more sincere and self-sacrificing patriotism, they are entitled to be supreme on the sea as they now are on land. We have no right to resent the challenge, but unless the ancestral blood flows less red in our veins we shall meet it with a heart no less firm than that with which our forefathers encountered the shock of the 'Invincible Armada'."

When Gabriel Princip fired his shots in Sarajevo, the challenge at once became immediate. If Germany and Austria were allowed to defeat Russia and France, Germany would unquestionably emerge supreme on the Continent. In London, Sir Edward Grey worked hard for peace, but he was at least equally anxious that, if war came, Britain should fight on the side of the Dual Entente.

Nevertheless, the British government was divided on the issue. The Prime Minister, H. H. Asquith, the Foreign Secretary, Grey, and the First Lord of the Admiralty, Winston

Churchill, were for supporting France, but at least three-quarters of the cabinet favoured neutrality, and as late as noon on August 2 it looked as though a majority of ministers would resign rather than be pushed into war. Before this could happen, word came that German troops were pouring across the Belgian frontier to strike at France. Britain, France, and Germany had all guaranteed Belgian neutrality, and on the morning of August 4 the British government sent an ultimatum to Berlin demanding that Germany honour this commitment. When the time limit of the ultimatum ran out at midnight, Britain declared war on Germany.

Few Canadians had believed that war would really come; the change of mood took nearly a week to develop. By the early evening of Tuesday, August 4, tense crowds had gathered in front of the bulletin boards of newspaper offices all across Canada. During the previous few days, as the European situation had steadily worsened, the crowds had grown continuously larger. When the bulletin was posted announcing that Britain had declared war on Germany, people in various Canadian cities reacted in much the same way. In Halifax they cheered themselves hoarse and waved their hats and handkerchiefs in the air; in Montreal they sang "La Marseillaise"; in Toronto the men spontaneously uncovered their heads and sang "God Save the King"; in Winnipeg a huge throng surged up and down Portage and Main streets, singing British patriotic airs and cheering; in Regina nine buildings believed to belong to Germans were set afire, and a crowd of 3,000 went "fighting mad" in front of the offices of the Regina *Morning Leader*; in Vancouver, where a Canadian Club convention was being held, the delegates rose three times in the course of the evening to sing "God Save the King".

Sir Robert Borden's cabinet experienced none of the strains that had divided Asquith's prior to the German attack on Belgium. Parliament had prorogued on June 12, and members and ministers had dispersed on vacation. However, between August 1 and August 4 the Canadian cabinet had met every day, but not to debate the issue of peace or war. The Canadian ministers discussed instead how they could best help the Mother Country, and the Minister of Militia offered an expeditionary force of 20,000 to 25,000 men to Britain.

6

At the time, this seemed a formidable undertaking and one that might well be the limit of the Canadian contribution.

Canada had taken no part in the diplomatic exchange that led to the conflict; she had not been consulted in the formulation of British policy or informed of its implications; and she was not expected to make any formal declaration of war. As Sir Wilfrid Laurier had told the House of Commons in January 1910, when he had been prime minister: "When Britain is at war, Canada is at war. There is no distinction." It was, however, well understood that the nature and extent of Canadian participation would be a matter for the Government of Canada to decide. Sir Robert Borden had no qualms on that score, and he certainly spoke for most Canadians. As early as August 1, 1914, he had cabled the Secretary of State for the Colonies in the name of the Governor General, the Duke of Connaught, that Canada would "make every sacrifice necessary to ensure the integrity and maintain the honour of our Empire".

In retrospect, it would seem that these were indeed the Canadian war aims, formulated in these terms before the German invasion of Belgium. At all events, no other war aims were ever seriously enunciated.* Before the invasion of Belgium not all Canadians had been convinced that the Empire was worth every sacrifice, but with the outbreak of war such doubts were suppressed. Only a few querulous voices spoke against Canada's sending troops to Europe, and it was generally accepted that republican France, imperial Britain, and tsarist Russia were fighting a just war against "the forces of militarism and autocracy" as represented by Germany and Austria-Hungary. Had it not been for Germany's criminal folly in invading neutral Belgium, a different view might have been taken, but in Canada, as in Britain, the remoter

---

* The myth of the German juggernaut had not been invented by 1914, for the very good reason that in both military and naval strength the Allies were overwhelmingly superior to the Central Powers, in quantity if not in quality. In August 1914, the Allies' standing armies totalled 2,238,000 as opposed to the Central Powers' 1,285,000; in army reserves the Allies had 12,000,000 against the Central Powers' 8,600,000; in naval strength the Allies had 80 battleships, 114 cruisers, 310 destroyers, and 115 submarines as opposed to the Central Powers' 52 battleships, 59 cruisers, 157 destroyers, and 31 submarines.

causes of the war were hidden by the leaping flames of Liège and Louvain, and the red glow from Belgium kindled anger even in those who had not previously shared the long-nurtured resentment and suspicion of Germany.

Perhaps more important even than imperial sentiment was the Canadian ignorance of the new nature of war. This ignorance, of course, was in no sense peculiarly Canadian. In Europe, too, the governments, general staffs, and people all thought in terms of a single great campaign across the summer countryside, of cavalry screens and wide-wheeling masses of manoeuvre, of Berlin taken before Christmas or Paris entered between harvest time and frost. Although most Canadians recognized that a European war would be on a grander scale than the previous conflict in South Africa, they were influenced, at least subliminally, by their memories of victory over the Boers. Then the Canadian contribution had been limited to a few thousand adventurous volunteers, only eighty-nine Canadians had been killed in action, and the patriotic excitement and economic benefits had seemed to more than compensate for the casualties. So does history bring in its roundabout revenges. Among the volunteers of the First Contingent in August 1914, the prevailing fear was that the fighting would be over before they could take part in it.

Even before August 4 Colonel Sam Hughes had been deluged with offers from militia units and individual volunteers anxious to go overseas. In 1911 a carefully prepared mobilization plan had been approved, but on July 31, Hughes, on his own initiative, ordered that this be disregarded. He preferred, he said, a different system, "really a call to arms, like the fiery cross passing through the Highlands of Scotland or the mountains of Ireland in former days". There was no time to substitute another mobilization scheme, but on August 6 the minister had a night lettergram sent direct to 226 Canadian militia units ordering them to take particulars of volunteers. As a result, the mobilization of the First Contingent was a thoroughly disorganized business, with many conflicting orders, counter-orders, and telephoned instructions emanating from Militia Headquarters.

Providentially, an interdepartmental conference at Ottawa

had begun work on Canadian government war planning on January 2, 1914, and had completed its task before the end of July. When the British Admiralty sent its Warning Telegram to Canadian Naval Service Headquarters on July 29, the agreed precautions were taken. The Royal Canadian Navy assumed control of all wireless stations and set up an examination service at defended ports but could do little about the general naval defence of the country. Canada had only two naval ships: the under-manned, ill-armed, light cruiser *Rainbow* on the West Coast, and the heavy cruiser *Niobe*, which was laid up at Halifax and would not be seaworthy for several weeks. The entire personnel strength of the navy consisted of fewer than 300 officers and men, less than half the number needed to crew the *Niobe*.

On the evening of August 4, the Canadian government placed the *Niobe* and the *Rainbow* "at the disposal of His Majesty for general service in the Royal Navy". Canada did what it could to assist the Royal Navy in manning the *Rainbow* and the *Niobe* as well as two submarines clandestinely purchased in Seattle shortly after the outbreak of war in defiance of the United States' neutrality laws.

An inquiry to the Admiralty by Prime Minister Borden on October 7, 1914, as to how Canada could co-operate in naval defence, brought the unenthusiastic response that nothing effective could be done, "as ships take too long to build", and that Canadian assistance should "be concentrated on [the] army". Canada undertook no naval shipbuilding until 1917, when the British Admiralty, faced with the submarine menace, hurriedly changed its mind and sent a panicky request for Canadian ships. Then a number of drifters and trawlers were constructed. During the war the total enrolment of officers and ratings in the Royal Canadian Navy was 1,471; some 600 Canadians joined the Royal Navy and the Royal Naval Reserve; and 7,360 joined the Royal Naval Canadian Volunteer Reserve. Among the latter enrolments were 73 surgeon probationers recruited from Canadian medical schools and 580 probationary flight lieutenants for the Royal Naval Air Service. The first Canadian casualties of the war were four young midshipmen lost with H.M.S. *Good Hope* at Coronel on November 1, 1914. During the course of the war the Royal Canadian Navy performed minesweeping operations at Halifax, patrolled Atlantic coastal waters and the St. Lawrence River, and undertook similar but even less extensive operations on the West Coast.

Before the war Canada had done nothing to establish a military aviation arm, but on August 25, 1914, Colonel Hughes cabled Lord Kitchener, the British Minister of War, that many Canadian and American aviators were offering their services. He received the reply that the British could use "six expert aeronauts" at once and that more might be required later. On September 16, Captain E. L. Janney was appointed commander of a provisional "Canadian Aviation Corps". Janney and Lieutenant W. F. N. Sharpe were sent to England with one aeroplane, but Sharpe was killed in a training accident, the aeroplane was lost somewhere in the British ordnance depots, Janney resigned his commission, and no more was heard of a "Canadian Aviation Corps" for nearly two years.

Nevertheless, more than 22,000 Canadians eventually joined the Royal Flying Corps and the Royal Naval Air Service, or the Royal Air Force, which was formed in April 1918 by the merger of the other two services. Most Canadians who flew in the war enlisted in Canada or transferred from the Canadian Expeditionary Force overseas, but some went to the United Kingdom on their own initiative. After 1916 the Royal Flying Corps and Royal Naval Air Service began large-scale recruiting in Canada, enlisting some 9,200 cadets for pilot and observer training and some 7,400 men for mechanic or ground training. Of these, 2,539 pilots and 85 observers were sent overseas. Before the war was over more than a quarter of the flying personnel in the British service were Canadians, as were many of the best Allied "aces".

However, if the Canadian government made little effort in naval or air matters, it did build up the army with a generous enthusiasm. On August 7 the Governor General, acting on information given him by Sam Hughes at a cabinet meeting, offered the British government on behalf of Canada four additional infantry battalions, one to be privately raised by Captain A. Hamilton Gault of Montreal, and one each to be raised by New Brunswick, Manitoba, and the city of Calgary.

New Brunswick promptly denied ever having made such an offer; Manitoba and Calgary found that the cost of infantry came higher than had been realized. Only Captain Gault's offer was actually implemented. He contributed, as he had promised, $100,000 towards the cost of raising and equipping a battalion of British ex-regulars that took the title "Princess Patricia's Canadian Light Infantry". In the same week the Dominion government gave one million bags of flour to Britain and the provinces made substantial gifts of oats, coal, potatoes, cheese, money, flour, horses, and canned salmon.

By August 18 volunteers began to arrive at Valcartier, the sandy area of waste ground sixteen miles northwest of Quebec City that Hughes had chosen as the place of concentration. By energy, improvisation, and the lavish expenditure of public funds, some sort of provision was made for the militia and the hundreds of patriotic young men who came at their own expense to Valcartier, clamouring to be enlisted. By September 8 Valcartier Camp held 32,665 soldiers.

The abandonment of the mobilization plan, which had been based on the existing militia organization, resulted in the formation at Valcartier of altogether new units – numbered battalions of a Canadian Expeditionary Force – with no regimental affiliation with the old Canadian militia units. In addition to the obvious disadvantages of organization and training that the new system entailed, the slight offered to the militia caused considerable bitterness and, in at least some cases, retarded the growth of regimental *esprit de corps.*

The selection of officers for the First Contingent was carried out at Valcartier by two military boards, but the Minister retained control over senior appointments himself and often interfered with the work of the boards even in the case of junior officers. Sam Hughes loved to take the salute at full-dress parades, a habit that would have interfered seriously with training had it not been that shortages of equipment, instructors, and organization made training virtually impossible in any case. After the Canadian government had been consulted and after Hughes had curtly rejected a number of suggested commanders for the Canadian Division, Lord Kitchener appointed Lieutenant-General E. A. H. Alderson, a

British regular officer and a South African veteran, to that post. Most senior appointments on the divisional and brigade staffs were filled in England by British officers.

In spite of repeated pleas from prominent French Canadians, no French-speaking unit was formed until November when Sir Wilfrid Laurier, by a personal appeal, obtained Borden's consent to the raising of a single French-Canadian battalion, the 22nd. At Valcartier those French-speaking recruits who were accepted were placed in English-speaking battalions.

Because the weather remained generally fine, the First Contingent experienced little hardship at Valcartier, although there were not enough tents or blankets to go round and for the first fortnight many men were without uniforms. After six weeks the Canadian Expeditionary Force was still relatively disorganized and almost totally untrained, but Valcartier certainly could not be used as a winter camp and Sam Hughes was fretting to get Canadian troops overseas. Towards the end of September preparations were hurriedly made to transport the force to England, and on the 23rd units began to embark. Typically, no loading tables were prepared, with the result that many units were split up and separated from their equipment, quantities of unit stores were left behind, and some ships were grossly overloaded while others sailed half empty.

The convoy assembled in Gaspé Basin where, on October 2, Colonel Hughes arrived in a rented tugboat. The Minister of Militia chugged noisily from ship to ship, handing out printed copies of his farewell speech to the troops. These were received without conspicuous enthusiasm, but the soldiers took Hughes seriously when he told them that this was their last chance to send letters home. The men gratefully handed down their mail, but when this was all collected it was placed aboard the last ship of the convoy and taken to England, whence it came back in the normal way.

When the First Contingent sailed from Gaspé Basin on October 3, it consisted of 1,424 officers and 29,197 other ranks. Of these, 18,495, or 62.5 per cent, had been born in the British Isles, and another 652, or 2.2 per cent, had been born in other British possessions. More than two-thirds of the officers were Canadian-born and practically all of them had been trained in the Canadian militia.

The voyage was uneventful, although on the last night out reports of German submarines in the English Channel caused the convoy to change its destination from Southampton to Plymouth. On October 14 when the transports dropped anchor in Plymouth Sound the soldiers lined the rails to gaze at the dreadnoughts riding at anchor in the harbour and to watch the searchlights of the Plymouth forts moving restlessly over the dark water. During the next five days the Canadians disembarked among cheering crowds and marched to Friary railway station where trains waited to take them to Salisbury Plain. In golden autumn weather, which lent an air of adventure to the whole undertaking, the troops swung past Stonehenge on their way to various camps on the plain. As they marched they sang, and by far the most popular song was the lilting "Tipperary", a pre-war music hall tune which had become a sort of unofficial march for all British troops.

No sooner had the Canadians arrived on Salisbury Plain than the weather became abominable. It rained on 89 of the 123 days between the middle of October and the middle of February. The training areas turned into quagmire; fuel was strictly rationed; hot water was scarce; and there were no facilities for drying wet clothing and blankets. Yet, in spite of outbreaks of influenza and meningitis, most of the young soldiers remained healthy, and even their most blasphemous comments on the wetness and the weather were generally salted with robust humour.

Some of the funniest things were said unintentionally, however, as when one infantry colonel, discovering a few of his men to be verminous, assembled the battalion and threatened the ultimate punishment. "I will never," he declared solemnly, "take a lousy man to France."

In spite of the weather on Salisbury Plain, the Canadians began serious training for the first time, and their eagerness to learn did much to compensate for the difficulties they encountered. Now, too, a good deal of shoddy Canadian equipment was replaced by items from British stocks. The soldiers soon found, for instance, that Canadian ammunition boots dissolved into grey pulp when wet, that Canadian uniforms

13

were sleazy, that the Bain wagon and Oliver equipment were useless, and that the "Sam Hughes shovel", part entrenching tool and part shield, was quite inadequate for either purpose. The Canadian war profiteer had obviously been as quick to offer his services as had the Canadian soldier.

The War Office decreed that a Canadian division should be formed from the First Contingent and that excess personnel be classified as reinforcements. At first no numerical designation was given to the Canadian division, but it became the 1st Canadian Division when a second division was formed. The First Contingent had no sooner sailed from Canada than the call went out across the Dominion for a second contingent of 20,000 men. The government also decided to keep an additional 30,000 men under arms in Canada as reinforcements, in addition to home defence units. In November the reinforcement quota was raised to 50,000. Again recruiting presented no problem, especially in the West where quotas were filled almost immediately. The Second Contingent, after spending the winter in local training areas, sailed for England in April, May, and June of 1915 and concentrated near Shorncliffe, Kent.

At the end of the first week of February the Canadian Division was ordered to prepare for a move. Like all soldiers everywhere in this war, the men welcomed any change. There always seemed a good chance that they could be no worse off somewhere else. In stormy weather between February 11 and February 15 the division crossed the Channel on small transports so crowded that the men had to take turns sleeping on deck and in the holds. On arriving at St. Nazaire on the Bay of Biscay they were issued with smelly goatskin coats, leather jerkins, and mitts for trench wear. They were given two days' rations of bully beef and hardtack – many soldiers supplemented this by buying "a yard of bread" which they carried under the straps of their packs – and were then crammed aboard dirty little French freight cars bearing the marking: "Hommes 40, Chevaux 8".

The war was now six months old and already it had solidified into a mutual siege of opposing trench lines running from Switzerland to the North Sea. In August 1914, the German armies had attacked in accordance with the "Schlieffen

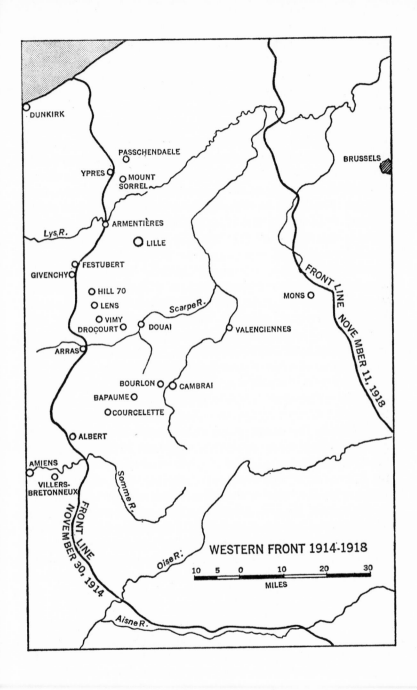

DUNKIRK

PASSCHENDAELE

YPRES
MOUNT
SORREL

BRUSSELS

Lys R.
ARMENTIÈRES

LILLE

FESTUBERT
GIVENCHY

HILL 70

LENS

VIMY
DROCOURT
DOUAI

Scarpe R.

MONS

FRONT LINE NOVEMBER 11, 1918

VALENCIENNES

ARRAS

BOURLON
CAMBRAI
BAPAUME
COURCELETTE

ALBERT

AMIENS
VILLERS-
BRETONNEUX

Somme R.

FRONT LINE NOVEMBER 30, 1914

Oise R.

WESTERN FRONT 1914-1918

10 5 0 10 20 30
MILES

Aisne R.

Plan" of 1905, which had called for a holding action against Russia in the east while a quick decision was sought against France in the west. For the sake of this brilliant but overbold plan Germany had invaded Belgium and brought the British Empire into the war against her.

And the Schlieffen Plan had failed. It had been modified, it is true, by the German commander-in-chief, Helmuth von Moltke, but it now seems possible that it might have failed even if it had been implemented as its originator, Graf von Schlieffen, had intended. Germany simply did not have enough troops for the wide-wheeling right wing that marched through Belgium. In any case, the advancing German armies had become disjointed; the right wing had been checked by the British at Le Cateau and by the French at Guise; and General von Kluck, the commander of the German First Army, had turned southeast to march across the front of Paris instead of behind it as the Schlieffen Plan had specified. Kluck had thus exposed his flank to a counter-stroke which had been promptly delivered at the First Battle of the Marne, and the German armies had retreated to the Aisne River, abandoning all hope of a quick and decisive victory.

The French Plan XVII had broken down even more ignominiously. The initial French drives into Alsace and Lorraine had been bloodily repulsed; a French force, advancing impetuously in the Ardennes, had been ambushed and hurled back; and by the end of August when the French high command awoke to the fact that its pre-war plan lay in utter ruin, the French army had lost some 200,000 men. By the end of 1914, after five months' fighting, French losses had climbed to about 800,000. The Allies' hopes that they would be saved by a Russian advance into East Prussia had been dashed when very much smaller German forces had disastrously defeated two Russian armies at Tannenberg and the Masurian Lakes.

In the west, after each side had failed to outflank the other in a series of westward moves that ended only at the sea, the front had become stagnant. The killing power of field artillery and machine guns, and the stopping power of barbed wire, forced both sides to dig. The soldiers began by scratching out shallow, grave-like shelters for themselves so that they could hide from the searing bits of metal that whined through the air, but soon elaborate trench systems appeared. The British Expeditionary Force of seven divisions had moved north to Flanders early in October, and bitter fighting followed about Ypres, but no appreciable change was made in the strategic situation. The British, however, found themselves committed to holding the "Ypres Salient", where their line bulged out for a few miles into the German trench system. For the next four years the Salient was to be a perpetual drain on British lives, but the thought of voluntarily abandoning ground for which so high a price had been paid was repugnant to the Allied high command.

This was the situation on the Western Front when the Canadians arrived to be initiated into the mysteries of trench warfare. They were to form a part of Lieutenant-General Sir H. W. Rawlinson's IV Corps of General Sir Douglas Haig's First Army and were to take over a portion of the front between the village of Aubers and the town of Armentières.

The long, circuitous journey from St. Nazaire to Flanders was uncomfortable, for there really was not room for forty fully equipped soldiers in one boxcar. As the trains ran through the leafless vineyards of France, the Canadians crowded at the partly open car doors to wave at civilians and to purchase bottles of wine and cognac at every halt. When they detrained east of Hazebrouck they could hear for the first time the sullen mutter of guns in the distance and could see the shimmer of gun-flashes reflecting from the low winter clouds over the front line.

When war had broken out seven months before, Canada had had only 3,110 regular soldiers, and few of these had found their way into the Canadian Expeditionary Force. By any reasonable professional standard, the officers and men who were now marching up to the line were no more than civilians in uniform.

On the afternoon of Thursday, April 22, 1915, most of the 18,000 Canadian soldiers in the Ypres Salient were lying in the bottom of their trenches, trying to catch some sleep. They had worked hard all night, filling sandbags, building breastworks, digging, and repairing barbed-wire entanglements. When they had relieved the French in the line the previous week they had been appalled by the condition of the shallow, inadequate trenches. Parados had not been built; filth was everywhere; rotting corpses were found buried in the parapets; huge rats, looking obscenely well fed, infested the crumbling dugouts; and the sickly sweet odour of death and corruption permeated the air.

Luckily, the front was quiet. The coppices and thorn hedges that still flourished near the battlefield were bursting into pale green leaf, and the sunny April days were warm with the promise of summer. Within two miles of the line red cattle were grazing in green fields and peasants were sowing their spring grain.

The Canadians had been relieved to find the Ypres Salient less dreadful than its reputation, for even in the spring of 1915 the place had a sinister name with the troops. In the long zigzag of trenches that ran across France and Belgium, the Salient bulged out eastwards into the German line like a small, rounded tumour, eight miles wide and six miles deep. On three sides it was dominated by higher ground in the possession of the enemy. In daylight, throughout its entire area, scarcely a man could move or a gun fire without being seen by the sharp eyes of German observation officers on the perimeter. The Salient, in fact, was "one huge artillery target" – and the Germans had a five-to-one superiority in guns.

However, since the Canadian Division had been in the line nothing much had happened. The German trenches, two or three hundred yards away, were only a jagged scar of sandbags and earthworks, silent, inoffensive, and seemingly deserted. Virtually the only evidence of war was that for the past two days a giant Krupp howitzer had been dropping 2,000-pound shells on Ypres, four and a half miles behind the front. By Thursday afternoon, a pall of red brick-dust and smoke hung over the ancient city, and all the roads leading westward from it were jammed with Belgian civilians fleeing with their carts, livestock, and household possessions.

At four o'clock that afternoon the Canadian sentries in the front line suddenly lifted their heads to listen. All at once the German artillery fire had intensified to a great drumbeat of sound, as the enemy gunners switched to the French trenches to the left. Soon the Canadians could distinguish the sharp answering bark of French 75's and the rattle of musketry. Sleeping men awoke and looked at each other, more in interest than apprehension. The French were being attacked.

The Canadians had not seen an attack before. Since their arrival in Flanders in February they had been in and out of the line several times without being involved in serious fighting. They were now holding a two-and-one-quarter-mile stretch of front in the very centre of the Salient between the three British divisions on their right and the French 45th Algerian and 87th Territorial divisions on their left. The eight battalions of the 2nd and 3rd brigades were responsible for holding the line, while the 1st Brigade was in reserve at the little village of Vlamertinghe, two and a half miles behind Ypres.

By half past four some shells began to fall on the Canadian trenches, but the main weight of fire was still on the French. At five o'clock a company commander of the 13th Battalion (Royal Highlanders of Canada), on the extreme left of the

Canadian line, climbed out of his trench to investigate. The first thing he noticed, without being able to account for it, was that the sun had a peculiar greenish tint; and then, as he gazed across to the French trenches, he witnessed a sight never before seen in the history of warfare. Between the German and French lines, extended for several hundred yards and moving slowly before a light wind, was a dense cloud of yellowish-green vapour. The Germans were using poison gas!

In the fields about Vlamertinghe the Canadians of the reserve brigade were playing football. Just before the supper hour they noticed that, mingled with the civilian refugees going by on the road, there were a few French and Algerian soldiers. Two French privates stopped beside the football field to tell the Canadians that "the Boche has broken through". A few minutes later French gun-teams began to go by, with a soldier on each horse and more soldiers riding on the limbers. Soon a steady stream of blue-coated *poilus* was passing through Vlamertinghe. Some choked and gasped for breath, some vomited, and some pointed to their throats and cried, "Gaz! Gaz!" All were definitely running away from the front.

General von Falkenhayn, the German commander-in-chief, had approved the use of gas more than three months previously, although it was specifically forbidden by the Hague Conventions of 1899 and 1906. He had decided to stand on the defensive in the west in 1915 while he struck an annihilating blow against Russia in the east, but in order to disrupt Allied plans he had sanctioned a certain number of limited offensive actions on the Western Front. The Ypres Salient was an obvious choice for such an attack. In February some 6,000 cylinders of chlorine had been allotted to the German Fourth Army, but unfavourable winds had prevented their use until April 22. In that interval the French and British had received at least four separate, independent, and detailed warnings that gas was to be used against them. Prisoners of war had said so; an Allied agent in Belgium had made the same report; and a German deserter had actually produced the gas mask he had been issued. Most Allied commanders had refused to believe it and the French high command had actually declared: "All this gas business need not be taken seriously."

20

As the chlorine cloud swept across no-man's-land to blanket the French lines to the left of the Canadians, the troops of the 45th Algerian Division broke and fled. A little later the 87th French Territorial Division farther left did the same. For a time the French 75's continued to fire, but before long even these fell silent as the French gunners joined in the rearward route, frequently abandoning their guns. The Germans were attacking almost due south across the chord of the Salient. By six o'clock a gap of more than four miles had been torn in the French line, and the grey-uniformed German infantry, advancing behind the gas with crude respirators over their faces, were threatening to cut off the entire Ypres Salient and surround the one Canadian and three British divisions still inside.

For a time the completeness of the French collapse, the surprise achieved by the Germans, and the disruption of telephone lines by the artillery bombardment prevented formation headquarters from learning exactly what the real situation was. Nevertheless, Lieutenant-General Alderson, the Canadian divisional commander, Lieutenant-General Sir H. C. O. Plumer, commander of V Corps, and General Sir Horace Smith-Dorrien, commander of Second Army, did what they could to fill at least part of the gaping hole in the Allied line. Throughout the Salient, reserve battalion buglers sounded the "Fall In", soldiers hastily paraded, rolls were called, and long columns were soon marching to the north and northeast.

At the front Brigadier-General R. E. W. Turner, V.C., commander of the 3rd Canadian Brigade, ordered his left-hand battalion, the 13th (Royal Highlanders of Canada), to extend its flank down the Poelcappelle–St. Julien road, and battalion commander Lieutenant-Colonel F. O. W. Loomis sent two companies north of St. Julien along the same road. Brigadier-General Arthur Currie, commander of the 2nd Canadian Brigade, with intelligent anticipation of orders, sent his 10th Battalion to support the 3rd Brigade and, after personally visiting his units, concentrated a battalion on Locality "C" on Gravenstafel Ridge, correctly appreciating that this was the vital ground in his area.

There were, of course, far too few men. The Germans were

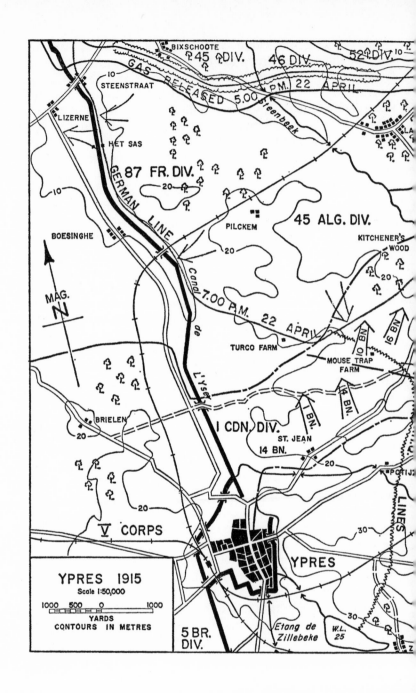

YPRES 1915
Scale 1:50,000

1000 500 0   1000
YARDS
CONTOURS IN METRES

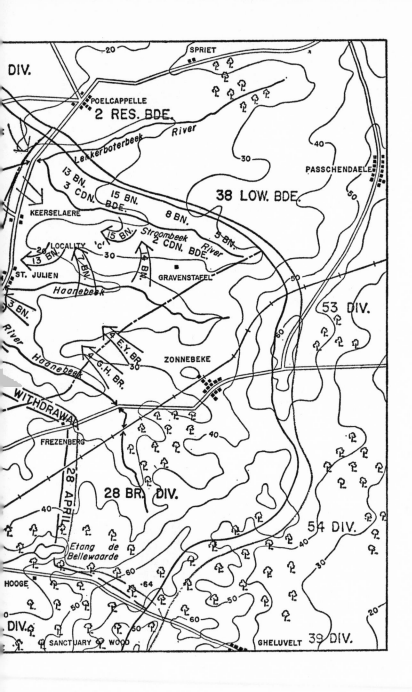

attacking with four corps of nearly eight divisions, and their infantry were sweeping triumphantly southwards across the chlorine-contaminated ground. Between the Canadians and the Yser Canal there was almost nothing to stop them. In this gap one Canadian field battery, the 10th, was deployed in an orchard north of St. Julien. The 18-pounders had been firing at the German trenches, but as the early April twilight began to close in a French sergeant who had rallied to the Canadian guns suddenly gripped the battery commander by the shoulder, pointed across a hedge, and cried: "Allemand!" The battery commander turned and to his amazement saw over the hedge, only two hundred yards away, the spiked helmets of a large body of German infantry who were moving down to attack St. Julien. It was the sort of target gunners dream of. A section of guns spun about and began to pump shells into the German column. The gun crews loaded and fired like men possessed, aiming over open sights at point-blank range. Within seconds the German dead lay in heaps upon the ground, and the survivors turned and ran, taking cover some distance away and digging in. Soon their rifle fire was whistling about the Canadian guns, bringing down showers of willow leaves from the near-by trees. Later that evening a party of sixty Canadian infantrymen arrived to protect the guns. With the infantry was nineteen-year-old Corporal Frederick Fisher of Montreal, a Colt machine-gunner of the 13th Battalion who manned his machine gun so bravely that he was awarded the first Canadian Victoria Cross of the war. He was killed the next day.

The German high command had erred on the side of caution in its plan for the attack. Only limited objectives had been set for April 22, for the enemy believed that merely by restricting the Salient he could force the Allies to evacuate it. Consequently, the advancing German troops stopped at 7.30 in the evening and began to dig in. Had they continued to exploit their success they would in all likelihood have captured Ypres and surrounded four British and Canadian divisions.

Some four hours after the gas had been released, Canadian Divisional Headquarters at the Château des Trois Tours ordered the first counterattack. Two battalions, the 10th and the 16th (Canadian Scottish), were told to retake Kitchener's Wood, a large oak plantation west of St. Julien. Of all the counterattacks that were to be launched during the Second Battle of Ypres, this one alone was operationally sound in its conception. Although its timing was somewhat later than the textbook definition of an "immediate" counterattack allows, this was compensated for by the fact that it was to be launched under cover of darkness and against an enemy who had had no time to prepare fixed defences. The objective, too, was well chosen, for Kitchener's Wood was an obvious jumping-off place for further German attacks. The two-battalion assault force was suitable, in the light of the size of the objective and the enemy strength.

Yet if the counterattack on Kitchener's Wood was operationally sound, its tactical execution was seriously at fault. In a field northeast of Mouse Trap Farm the soldiers formed up silently, tense and excited. By the light of a low and cloudy moon they could just make out the dark outline of the wood a thousand yards ahead. In response to whispered instructions, some 1,500 men finally stood in eight ranks at intervals of thirty yards, massed shoulder to shoulder in the attack formation they had practised in training camp. It was a formation that might have been used at Waterloo, before the magazine rifle or machine gun had been thought of. Canon F. G. Scott, an enthusiastic padre, moved through the waiting ranks, shaking hands with the men and exclaiming over and over again: "A great day for Canada, boys! A great day for Canada!"

At fifteen minutes before midnight the order to advance was given and the silent mass of men stepped out into the darkness, bayonets fixed and rifles at the port. The only sound was the muffled tramp of feet and the slapping of empty scabbards against thighs. Half the distance to the wood had been covered when a single Very light spluttered up from the German lines, to be followed by a shower of flares that instantly turned the battlefield as light as day. The massive Canadian phalanx was an ideal target. As enemy machine guns ripped out and rifles crackled, a flickering line of fire showed up against the outline of the wood. The Canadians fell in swaths, but after an instant's hesitation the whole lumbering mass let out a cheer and ran forward. Officers shouted encouragement to their men, who replied with the high-pitched, excited scream characteristic of bayonet charges. They poured through the inadequate German wire and into the trench that ran along the southern edge of the wood. Few Germans waited to receive them; those who did were killed with bayonet or butt; and a minute later the attackers pressed on into the dark wood.

Here no man could see more than a few feet in front of him, for the moon had set and the night was black among the trees. Vague shapes in the shadows might be either friend or foe. By now most officers of both battalions had been killed or wounded, and about half the soldiers. All cohesion was lost as excited men pushed on in search of an enemy to kill. In the middle of the wood the Canadians were surprised to find the huge black shapes of the guns of the 2nd London Heavy Battery which had been overrun and captured a few hours previously. By the gun position, tethered to a tree and holding up a shattered leg in mute appeal, stood a dejected-looking horse.

Divisional headquarters was told at 2.45 A.M. that Kitchener's Wood had been recaptured, but in fact some determined Germans with machine guns were still holding out in organized positions. Their fire was so galling that by four o'clock the remaining Canadians, now only some 500 of the original 1,500, fell back to the trench south of the wood and prepared to make a stand there.

Dawn came, cold as an anticlimax; the eastern sky grew grey; and soon there was enough light to see the battlefield of the night before. Back across the open fields lay the Canadian dead and wounded, heaped in grisly piles or laid out in long rows where the enfilade fire of machine guns had cut them down like corn. The coloured kilts of the 16th Battalion showed up brightly beside the khaki forms of the 10th Battalion's dead. Some of the bodies still moved, twitching and writhing from time to time as pain recurred. Rescue attempts were made, but had to be abandoned in the face of German fire.

The counterattack in mass formation had failed with terrible loss. Later – much later – the troops would be taught to attack in open order, maintaining the momentum of the assault by judicious reinforcements of success. They would learn (but at how high a cost for the lesson!) to consolidate in stages, to bring defensive stores with them in the third or fourth wave, to maintain communication with a single co-ordinating headquarters, and to hoard a reserve against the unforeseen. Now they knew none of these things and so paid the price of their ignorance.

With impeccable military logic, the German high command still believed that when the Allies found their position in the Salient seriously constricted they would evacuate it. Accordingly, the enemy made no offensive move on April 23. Nevertheless, this was a bad day for the Canadian Division and the British battalions sent to reinforce it. The Allied high command did not for a moment consider abandoning the Salient, although the gap between the original Canadian left flank and the Yser Canal had still to be closed. If this purely defensive task had been made the single aim of operations, it might have been achieved without excessive loss. However, back in the more tranquil atmosphere of Cassel, thirty miles behind the Salient, General Sir John French, the British commander-in-chief, met with General Ferdinand Foch, the commander of all French armies from south of Arras to the sea, and agreed to co-operate in counterattacks to restore the original front.

An attack by one company of the 2nd (East. Ontario) Battalion against the German strong-point in the southwest corner of Kitchener's Wood failed at dawn, when the ground mist suddenly lifted to reveal the advancing Canadians to a well-entrenched enemy 200 yards away. Within seconds the German machine guns wiped out practically the entire company. Only fifteen survivors managed to crawl back to shelter in the 10th Battalion's trench.

Even more disastrous was a counterattack launched that morning by the 1st and 4th battalions aided by two companies of the 3rd Middlesex Regiment. The orders were to drive the enemy from Mauser Ridge, a low hill about a mile north of the village of Wieltje. As dawn broke, the Canadians on Hill Top Ridge, 1,500 yards south of Mauser Ridge, could plainly see the Germans wiring their position across the valley. The ground between was smooth, gently rolling countryside, virtually devoid of cover. The only artillery support available for this attack was eight light field guns and eight 4.5-inch howitzers, and these guns were incapable of bringing down anything like an adequate amount of neutralizing fire.

The 1st and the 4th battalions lined up "in most perfect order as if on parade" and at the given word began their long walk towards Mauser Ridge. They passed a farmhouse where the farmer's supper lay untouched on the kitchen table, went through a meadow where cows lowed for someone to milk their swollen udders, and then, still in perfect order, went over the slight rise of Hill Top Ridge and came into view of the enemy. They were at once met by a hurricane of fire from German machine guns, rifles, and artillery. At every step dozens of men fell, but the remainder plodded resolutely on to fall in their turn. Some actually reached the bottom of the valley where a line of pollard willows grew, but here they stopped. They were still 600 yards away from the nearest German, and it was pitifully obvious that no one could climb the slope ahead and live. The remnants of the two battalions lay down on the ground after an action that had been as gallant, and as insane, as the charge of the Light Brigade. The day's fighting cost the 1st Battalion 404 casualties and the 4th Battalion 454.

While this was going on, other troops had been moved up to close, at least partly, the hole in the Allied line. Two companies of the 3rd Battalion (The Toronto Regiment) had taken up position near St. Julien; the 2nd Battalion, the 7th (British Columbia) Battalion, the 14th Battalion (Royal Montreal Regiment), and the 15th Battalion (48th Highlanders of Canada) were also deployed, and a group of fresh British units were stationed immediately east of the Yser Canal. Before the battle was over a total of thirty-three British battalions were placed under the Canadian Division – by itself an indication of how little effective control was exercised by higher formations, for a divisional headquarters was equipped to control a maximum of sixteen battalions. So desperate was the situation that commanders had to use whatever units they had to hand. Battalions were divided, placed under other brigade headquarters and employed in other brigade areas. Fortunately, the Germans were not able to attack in force on April 23 – the completeness of their success was more than they had bargained for. The German supreme command had seen no more in their attack than an opportunity to test a new weapon and for this failure of imagination they were to pay dearly. Now they had no reserves immediately ready to throw in.

At 1.20 in the afternoon the 1st and 3rd brigades received a priority message from the Canadian Division: "French report that Germans are apparently running short of ammunition. They have been ordered to seize this opportunity to push forward." At his headquarters at Mouse Trap Farm, Brigadier-General Turner scribbled a bitter little note on this message: "An example of the value of information received from the rear."

In fact, the French did not push forward or even attempt to do so. Since they had lost much of their artillery, this was a sensible decision, although it would have been better if General Foch's headquarters and the French commanders on the spot could have arrived at a common policy in this regard. As it was, Foch, obsessed by the offensive spirit that was to erase the shame of 1870, breathed fire and slaughter at Cassel. He promised the British commander-in-chief great assaults, and presumably he ordered them, but his orders were prudently disobeyed.

That afternoon, however, General Headquarters ordered six British battalions to counterattack across exactly the same ground that was now dotted with the dead and wounded of the 1st and 4th battalions. Since nothing had been done to silence the enemy's fire, the result was predictable. The Germans were not, after all, running short of ammunition. The British attack was cut down just as the Canadian had been, and each of the assaulting battalions lost about half of its officers and between 200 and 425 men. The bare northern slopes of Hill Top Ridge were littered with little khaki clumps. Nightfall found the surviving attackers, hopelessly intermingled, confused, and almost completely officerless, digging in – still some 600 yards from Mauser Ridge.

Even if the French had co-operated in this counterattack

as Foch had promised, there was no possible hope of success. How could the British, with a serious inferiority in men and guns, hope to cross that bullet-swept ground and push the enemy off his position? Obviously there had been no rational appreciation of the situation by the headquarters that ordered the attack, and equally obviously there had been no on-the-spot reconnaissance. Just as pernicious was the fact that there had been no protest against a stupid order by the officers who actually were in a position to look across from Hill Top Ridge to Mauser Ridge and who could therefore see the futility of the whole affair.

As soon as darkness fell, the work of bringing in the wounded began in earnest. An advanced dressing station had been set up in a red-brick *estaminet* in Wieltje, and there, by the dim light of lamps and candles, doctors and medical staff laboured in their shirt-sleeves, their hands and forearms covered with blood. The place reeked like a slaughterhouse, but in spite of the unremitting work of the doctors the long rows of stretcher cases in the courtyard seemed never to diminish. At the aid post established in the stables of Mouse Trap Farm the wounded lying on straw in the courtyard could hear bullets striking the other side of the stable wall. When the Germans shelled the farm, the farmhouse caught fire, as did the straw on which the wounded were lying. A dump of 200,000 rounds of rifle ammunition began to explode; the shelling continued; and the whole place was filled with flame, lyddite fumes, and flying bullets. Through this inferno the medical staff calmly rescued the wounded.

By nightfall of April 23 some sort of line had been re-established, a line with many gaps in it still, but one that was nevertheless capable of being defended. A total of twenty-one and one-half battalions (twelve of them Canadian) now faced forty-two German battalions. The Germans had not advanced appreciably during the day, but everyone from private to general knew that another attack was bound to come.

That night the Salient throbbed with urgency. Men who had fought desperately all day worked desperately all night. Parapets had to be strengthened, sandbags filled, traverses built, signal wire repaired. The shelled roads were packed with traffic, as ammunition, reinforcements, and rations moved up to the front and laden ambulances moved back. Near the bridges across the Yser Canal the noise of wheels and hooves on the *pavé* was a continuous rolling thunder that almost drowned out the sound of the guns. Until half past two the night was silvery with moonlight, and in the southwest sky the red flames shooting up from the burning city of Ypres outlined the black ruin of the old Cloth Hall.

The enemy, too, worked all night long. When it became evident that the British intended to cling stubbornly to their highly vulnerable position, the German commander, Duke Albrecht of Württemberg, ordered two converging attacks, one to drive south to Vlamertinghe across the Yser Canal, while the other struck the Canadian front, captured St. Julien, and squeezed out all the northern portion of the Salient. Twenty fresh German battalions were brought up to the front to strengthen the assault that was to go in at dawn.

Long before daybreak the Canadians were standing to in their trenches. There was nothing to see in the darkness except a few faraway stars in a black sky, and nothing to hear except a mutter of German guns to the west. An icy wind blew across no-man's-land towards the Canadians, who gripped their rifle stocks in numbed fingers and shivered with cold and weariness.

They had been standing to for half an hour when three signal rockets, two red and one green, burst in the sky above the village of Pilckem. Everyone tensed, wondering whether this was the signal for battle, but nothing else happened. Then at four o'clock three red flares floated down from a German balloon anchored over Westroosebeke. These had hardly spluttered out before the Canadian trenches were deluged with a sudden rain of shellfire. At the apex of the Canadian front, sentries of the 8th (Winnipeg) Battalion and the 15th Battalion (48th Highlanders of Canada) saw a line of ghostly figures, wearing mine-rescue helmets, climb over the enemy parapet. The Germans held hoses in their hands and from these issued a cloud of greenish-yellow vapour that drifted slowly across no-man's-land. As it billowed across the Canadian line, men began to cough and choke, tears blinded them, and many suffocated in agony as they slipped to the bottom of a trench where the gas concentration was densest. Then the bombardment ceased as suddenly as it had begun and waves of German infantry leapt from their trenches and started forward.

The right company of the 8th Battalion, which had escaped the gas, was able to bring heavy enfilade fire to bear on the attackers. Elsewhere the Canadians fought as best they could. The Winnipeg men had been provided with dampened cotton bandoliers to hold over their faces; others made do with moistened handkerchiefs. Neither precaution was of much use against the biting chlorine gas. When the 8th Battalion called for artillery support, the guns replied promptly, but the 15th Battalion was told that its supporting artillery was out of range and could not help.

Nevertheless, ragged rifle fire cracked out along the entire front as the Germans came on. Thanks to Sam Hughes, the Canadians were equipped with the Ross rifle, which, although an excellent target weapon, could not stand the stress of rapid fire. In the far-off days of peace there had been considerable debate about the defects of this rifle. Indeed, expert opinion had foretold exactly what was now to happen. But Sam Hughes, as always, had known best and had gone up against opposition as a kite rises against the wind. Finally it had reached the point where anyone who spoke against the Ross as a service weapon had become Hughes's personal enemy. Canadian soldiers were now to pay with their lives for the personality of the Minister of Militia and Defence. This morning the Rosses jammed repeatedly, and the soldiers tried desperately to work the bolts loose with their boot heels and the handles of entrenching tools. The wounded, lying in the bottom of the trenches, loaded fresh rifles and handed them up to their comrades on the firing-step.

Incredibly, the first German attack was stopped in its tracks, except in the centre of the line where the survivors of the 15th Battalion's right-hand company had to withdraw a few hundred yards. However, the enemy guns opened up again when the German infantry halted, and the entire Canadian line from the apex to St. Julien was saturated with shells. The next attack forced the 15th Battalion to fall back some 700 yards. By now only a handful of the Highlanders were left – the day's work cost the battalion 647 casualties. No other Canadian unit in the entire war suffered so heavily in so short a time.

Brigadier-Generals Turner and Currie threw in what reserves they had. Companies of the 5th and 7th battalions were placed under the 8th Battalion, and the 10th Battalion was moved up from its trench south of Kitchener's Wood to support the battered line. By now all that was left of the 10th Battalion was three officers and 171 men.

All morning the German attacks continued with undiminished fury, but after five and a half hours of fighting it was apparent that they had fallen far short of their objectives. Although the Canadians had been pushed back a thousand yards over half a mile of front, the breach had been sealed off and the defenders were fighting as bravely as ever. Nevertheless, the Germans still came on, with very superior numbers, and the Canadian reserves who might have been thrown in to hold the line were – all too many of them – lying in the open fields in front of Kitchener's Wood or on the bare forward slopes of Hill Top Ridge. At eleven o'clock the 7th (British Columbia) Battalion and the 14th and 15th battalions withdrew 300 yards to a new position behind Gravenstafel Ridge. During this retirement the two left-hand companies of the British Columbians were overrun. St. Julien was now open to attack from three sides.

Although there were further fighting retirements during the afternoon, the hard-pressed line never broke. When St. Julien finally fell, the two companies of the Toronto Regiment holding out there were overwhelmed. Only forty-three men escaped, almost all of them wounded and two of them totally blind. Shortly after midnight British reinforcements began to arrive in strength, and the situation was stabilized.

The next morning five British battalions under Brigadier-General C. P. A. Hull were ordered to counterattack towards St. Julien and Kitchener's Wood. As they moved out from their start line north of Mouse Trap Farm, German machine-gun and rifle fire cut them down in long, regular rows. Looking through his field glasses, an inexperienced staff officer at Mouse Trap Farm inquired: "Why do they stop?" The reply was: "They are dead." The attack was everywhere brought to a halt far short of the objective. In a few minutes the five battalions lost 73 officers and 2,346 other ranks.

On the evening of April 25, three fresh British divisions arrived to reinforce the Salient. The exhausted Canadian infantry, who had fought so magnificently, were pulled out of the line during the 26th. The Second Battle of Ypres continued sporadically for another three weeks (and Princess Patricia's Canadian Light Infantry were heavily engaged with the 28th British Division at Frezenberg Ridge), but the German chance of a breakthrough had long since disappeared. It had disappeared between April 22 and April 24 when the Canadians had held the line and refused to admit defeat.

Time and again the British loyally launched counterattacks in which the French were pledged to co-operate, only to find that the promised French participation did not materialize. These counterattacks, like all of their predecessors except the Canadian night assault on Kitchener's Wood, were operationally unsound. Unrealistic objectives were chosen, artillery preparation was quite inadequate, the routes were suicidal, and, indeed, in nothing except in timing could any of the assaults be considered as true "deliberate" counterattacks. The result was that at Second Ypres, unlike most other battles, the defenders suffered considerably heavier casualties than did the attackers. The British Army, including the Canadians, lost nearly 60,000 men in the whole battle.

At last General Smith-Dorrien suggested a partial withdrawal from Ypres Salient, for, he said, "I am doubtful if it is worth losing any more men to regain this French ground unless the French do something really big." There can be no doubt that the British would have been far better off if they had evacuated the Salient, for its retention made no military sense at all. The area was no more than a large killing-ground where the British forces were eventually to lose more than half a million men. Yet because of his eminently sensible suggestion that it would be wise to retire to a shorter and more easily defended line, Smith-Dorrien was forced to resign his command. And thus – as so often in this war – one of the principal results of Canadian heroism was the opposite of what had been intended. The Canadians had saved the Salient – to their own most grievous loss in the years to come.

The Second Battle of Ypres was to be the only major defensive operation in which the Canadians were engaged in the First World War. The casualties of the Canadian Division had been appalling: 66 officers and 1,784 other ranks killed; 122 officers and 3,289 other ranks wounded; and 776 taken prisoner – a total of 6,037 out of a front-line infantry strength of about 10,000. Nevertheless, those who survived had the enduring satisfaction of knowing that in their first time of trial they had done far more than could possibly have been expected of them. They had withstood the assault of greatly superior forces and had not broken even when attacked by the terrible new weapon of poison gas. Their stand had saved the British divisions in the Salient from being cut off and annihilated, a reverse that might have changed the course of the entire war.

Both sides made grave mistakes in handling the battle, but they were, significantly, quite different kinds of mistakes. The Germans failed strategically, through a lack of imagination. The surprise of poison gas, if it had been correctly exploited, could conceivably have broken the trench deadlock and won the war in the West. It had been Germany's first chance to achieve this since September 1914, and it was not to come again, except briefly in March of 1918. In the future both sides were to use gas – and more deadly gas than chlorine – but once the element of surprise had gone all hopes of a breakthrough vanished. The German mistakes all flowed from this basic failure of strategic imagination – the lack of reserves to exploit success, the too-limited choice of objectives on April 22, the timing of the initial attack too late in the day to make sweeping gains possible before last light. In other respects the Germans fought the battle well, and they were even very quick to recognize and correct their earlier error. The attack they launched on the morning of April 24, had it been the initial attack, would almost certainly have pinched out the Salient.

The Allied errors, on the other hand, were committed at each level – strategic, operational, and tactical – and were persisted in throughout the entire course of the battle. In the first place, the Allies should not have been in the Salient at all. The reasons given for hanging grimly on to this bloodstained patch of low ground do not survive intelligent analysis. "Political considerations" were said to be involved. This meant that a portion of Belgium remained unoccupied, and to put it thus bluntly is to expose the ridiculousness of the argument. Strategically, the Allied planners claimed that the possession of the Salient blocked a German advance to the Channel ports, but this advance could have been blocked far better a few miles farther back where the defenders could have held a shorter and stronger line. Finally, it was claimed that the Salient could be a jumping-off place for an Allied offensive to roll up the German left flank. It was, in fact, so used in the latter half of 1917 at the Third Battle of Ypres, which is better known as Passchendaele, and the results of that battle should forever conclusively silence this particular plea for the retention of the Salient.

But if the Salient, against all military logic, was going to be held, it should at least have been defended by the forces of a single nation. The joint between the French and the British armies should never have been allowed to fall in so vulnerable an area. If – again against all military logic – the joint was to be where in fact it was, much better liaison arrangements should have been in force and at much lower levels of command. Finally, when in the course of the actual battle the two French divisions on the north had fled, there should have been no effort *permanently* to retain what was left of the Salient, narrower, more cramped, and much more vulnerable even than it had originally been. Every effort should have been made to withdraw the threatened British and Canadian formations to the chord, which, incidentally, should have been prepared in advance against such an eventuality.

A frequent complaint against Allied generalship in the First World War is that senior commanders made their plans from the map without ever looking at the actual ground. It is, God knows, a complaint that can be all too readily documented. However, at the Second Battle of Ypres it would almost seem as though the commanders did not even look at the map.

The almost total disregard of the repeated warnings that the Germans were to use poison gas was in keeping with the general mismanagement of the battle. Additional aerial reconnaissance, which was quite feasible at this stage of the war, or trench raids might well have confirmed the existence of the gas cylinders. Even without such confirmation the reports were sufficiently strong and converging to have required that the troops be informed. There was little they could have done to protect themselves physically, but forewarning would at least have lightened the psychological terrors of the unknown.

Enough has already been said about the failure of the counterattacks. Two of the cardinal maxims of sound planning are that commanders should always ask the maximum from their troops and that they should never ask the impossible. At Second Ypres the impossible was demanded again and again. The reasons for this go much deeper than any mere tactical analysis can reveal. Subordinate commanders at every level of command were allowed far too little discretion in the execution of orders, and there was far too little feedback of ideas and assessments up the chain of command. This was a fault built into the system. One might almost say that it was a fault built into the society that had produced the system. "Discipline," said British Field Service Regulations, "is the prompt, willing and implicit obedience of orders." The final adjective is the trouble there, for it tends to make discipline a mechanical rather than a spiritual thing.

At the purely Canadian level – that is, at the brigade level and below – there were fewer errors, possibly because there was less scope for them. There were indeed some serious lapses in the staff work of General Turner's 3rd Brigade, lapses that were to bode ill for the future. The mass formation adopted for the attack on Kitchener's Wood was, in the light of hindsight, deplorable, but the Canadian battalions had learned no other method of conducting a night assault. Offsetting these mistakes was Currie's splendid handling of his brigade and his sharp tactical eye for ground. His shrewd decision to defend Locality "C" as vital ground contained at least the germ of an idea that the Allies never fully developed during the war, the idea of all-round, as opposed to linear, defence. It was, unfortunately, left to Ludendorff and von Lossberg to refine this concept, which they did in the autumn of 1917.

All in all, the Second Battle of Ypres should be remembered by those latter-day apologists who protested that the "new" form of trench warfare and the introduction of "new" defensive weapons like the machine gun do much to excuse the failings of Allied generalship in the First World War. Here the Allies were not attacking but defending, and they were saved from utter disaster only by the wonderful fighting qualities of their troops. In this regard there is a paradox that is worth noting: from the brigade level down, the Canadians were, by and large, amateur soldiers, raw, green, and untrained; at the higher levels, commanders and staffs were British professionals who had presumably studied war as a career; yet it was the amateurs who saved the situation and the professionals who came close to throwing it away. This was not because amateur soldiers possess some magic secret that is hidden from the professionals, although a few military critics have drawn that conclusion. By and large, and other things being equal, the professional should beat the amateur in war, just as he does in sports. The trouble was that by 1914 the command and staff fabric of the British regular army had stiffened into a sort of Byzantine formalism.

After the battle, messages of congratulation poured in to the Canadian Division from all over the world, and in his official dispatch Sir John French reported that the Canadians' "gallantry and determination undoubtedly saved the situation". They had indeed won a reputation as fighting men second to none in the world, but more important to the troops was what they had learned about themselves. The Second Battle of Ypres, confused, agonized, and tragic though it was, gave the Canadians an *esprit de corps* they never lost.

General Sir Douglas Haig, the commander of First British Army, was a stony-eyed Lowland Scot with a carefully clipped moustache and an aggressively out-thrusting jaw. The immaculate correctness of his dress was an example to all who saw him and the mirror-bright shine of his riding boots the despair of the staff officers who tried to emulate him. For some reason those who disliked Haig were inclined to be quite irrationally irritated by his sartorial perfection. When Lloyd George was Britain's prime minister, he used to remark caustically that "Haig is brilliant to the top of his boots".

Years before the war, when Haig was single and unknown, he had had the reputation of being both bad-tempered and obstinate. Since then, he had managed to curb the first of these faults admirably, at least on most occasions. His rare flashes of anger were therefore the more impressive. He may have been aware of this. Certainly when he visited the headquarters of the Canadian Division at nine o'clock on the morning of May 22, 1915, he made no attempt to conceal his displeasure. He sat at a small table in General Alderson's office and soundly berated the Canadian commander and the four staff officers who were lined up in front of him. In the words of a British officer who was present, Haig lectured them "like a pack of schoolboys" for the Canadians' failure to capture all the objectives First Army had set five days previously. The Army Commander "stormed" and "raged" and "poured scorn on the efforts of the Canadians".

Alderson, who was a reasonable man and a better than average soldier, did his best to defend his troops. Quietly he pointed out that the enemy was much superior in artillery, that almost all the British guns were light fieldpieces which were of little use against German strong-points, that the sector where the Canadians had had to attack was difficult and water-logged, and that the enemy defences were very strong. Haig impatiently brushed these arguments aside. He had ordered that ground be captured and captured it must be. With sufficient "pluck" and determination the objectives could be taken. The attacks were to continue. And having said this he curtly took his leave, climbed back into his staff car, and drove off to his own headquarters in the rear.

From one point of view, Haig's bad temper was natural, if misdirected. May had not been a successful month for the First Army. Or indeed for the Allies as a whole. Early in the month the French had launched a great offensive against Vimy Ridge, but after a six-day battle which had cost them 100,000 casualties they had got no more than part way up the slope. The British had been cajoled into launching "diversionary" assaults to keep the Germans from reinforcing Vimy Ridge, but on the 9th, when successive waves of British and Indian troops had attacked at Aubers Ridge, they had been cut down by withering machine-gun and artillery fire and had lost 11,000 men in twelve hours for no gain of ground. Haig, not unduly discouraged, had decided to try the same thing again, this time between Neuve Chapelle and the village of Festubert, north of the La Bassée Canal. On the night of May 15–16 the 2nd British and the 1st Indian divisions had made slight gains at a heavy cost in casualties, but the enemy had merely withdrawn a few hundred yards to a new line.

Not for the last time in the war, Haig had immediately leapt to the conclusion that this tactical withdrawal to a better position was a sign that German resistance was crumbling. Why else would any soldier give up a foot of ground? He decided to reinforce success. He ordered a new attack for May 18, and in spite of the fact that less than three weeks previously the Canadian Division had lost nearly two-thirds of its fighting strength at the Second Battle of Ypres, he ruled that the next assault near Festubert would be made by the 3rd Canadian Brigade and the 4th Guards Brigade. Zero hour was set for 4.30 in the afternoon, when everyone, including the enemy, could see exactly what he was doing.

Haig, however, did not issue his orders for the assault until 1.55 P.M., and, as a consequence, by the time they had percolated down through Corps and Division to the 3rd Brigade it was already almost time for the attack. The supporting bombardment, which should have begun at 2.30, could not start until 3.30, and the Canadian assault could not be launched until 5.25. By then the 4th Guards Brigade on the left had already been stopped dead by German machine guns and the enemy had been thoroughly alerted.

Brigadier-General Turner, commander of the 3rd Brigade, had planned the attack with the 14th Battalion (Royal Montreal Regiment) on the left, and the 16th (Canadian Scottish) Battalion on the right. The objective was a road called La Quinque Rue, northwest of a German defended locality known as "the Orchard".

The area about Festubert was a perfectly flat, alluvial plain, inadequately drained by three sluggish streams and innumerable tributary ditches. As was their unsporting custom, the Germans held what high ground there was, and from the Canadian trenches even bold observers, lifting their heads higher than was safe, could obtain only a limited view of the battlefield. Within a hundred yards or so the monotonous horizon closed down, encircling a patch of mud littered like a junkyard with the debris of war. Since the water table lay only two feet below the surface of the soil, the front line was a mere scratch in the ground and the sandbag breastworks did not provide protection against rifle bullets. To make matters worse, the 1/10,000 and 1/50,000 scale trench maps issued to the troops were incredibly inaccurate. Road junctions, buildings, and strong-points were sometimes wrongly plotted by as much as 450 yards. Moreover, these maps had thoughtfully been printed with south at the top and east to the left, which inverted co-ordinate readings and made memorization and orientation extremely difficult. A neat, new, military-looking system had been devised for designating features on these maps – everything was given a number and a letter. The result was a cartographer's nightmare where U2, K5, L8, or P9 might be a trench, a house, a hedge, a ditch, a machine-gun post, or nothing at all. The infantry found it impossible to identify some localities and the artillery were even harder put to it to provide accurate supporting fire.

In the late afternoon of May 18 the two Canadian battalions assembled in the fields near Indian Village and then, with the sinking sun behind them, advanced across a maze of ditches, trenches, and water-filled shell holes that broke up their formations and often led to dangerous crowding. As soon as the attackers left their trenches they came under heavy observed fire, from both small arms and artillery. A single salvo of whiz-bangs killed or wounded forty-seven Highlanders in one 16th-Battalion company, and on the left the Montreal men were pinned to the ground 400 yards from their start line. An orderly from the Wiltshire Regiment, through which the 14th Battalion was passing, came back to his major's dugout and reported: "The Canadians are all blown to hell. There is terrible murder up there."

It was not an inaccurate description. Nevertheless, on the right the 16th-Battalion companies, making their own plans on the spot, pressed on to La Quinque Rue where they halted for the night. Rain fell in sheets all through the hours of darkness, soaking the living and the dead and tantalizing the wounded who lay in the wet mud, felt the chill raindrops fall, and begged aloud for water. On the Royal Montreal Regiment's front the consolidating platoons of No. 3 Company watched with apprehensive pride while their fifteen-year-old bugler, Anthony Ginley, twice guided parties of stretcher-bearers up to no-man's-land. That night, even after a wounded man was located, it took four hours to carry him back to the dressing station at Indian Village.

The grey morning light revealed an appalling scene. Dead bodies lay everywhere, most of them clad in khaki. Some knelt in front of the German wire where they had been killed before taking the leap across it, some hung over ditches, some lay in long rows where a machine gun had caught them in enfilade. The decomposed corpses of those who had been killed the previous autumn sprawled in the shell holes where they had crept to die; some were almost skeletons now, their white bones picked clean by rats. A 14th-Battalion diarist recorded: "We had to walk over dead bodies and sleep beside them." Smashed rifles and bloodstained equipment lay scattered about the ground and the stench of death was everywhere.

On the night of May 18–19 the 2nd Canadian Brigade came into the line on the right of the 3rd Brigade. Haig grouped the Canadian Division, the 51st Highland Division, and the artilleries of the British 2nd and 7th divisions under General Alderson to form "Alderson's Force", which was really a corps, but without a corps headquarters or staff. In addition to commanding this "Force", General Alderson also had to exercise direct command over the Canadians. The experiment was not a success.

The enemy, willing to fight it out on these lines for as long as might be required, reinforced his front about Festubert, but the Canadians were ordered to attack again on May 20. The men who had survived Second Ypres now had intimate knowledge of war and they were less inhibited in expressing their opinions than British regular officers might have been. The front-line battalion commanders, supported by their brigadiers, wanted to delay the assault until it could be launched under cover of darkness, but they were overruled. Perhaps the senior commanders, who had studied war at the staff college in leisurely Victorian or Edwardian days, remembered being told that only highly trained regular troops could be trusted to carry out a night attack. Certainly none of the directing staff solutions at Camberley had stressed the stopping power of aimed machine-gun fire. The Canadian Division was peremptorily ordered to attack once more in broad daylight. The 2nd Brigade was to capture an enemy strong-point known as K5 and the 3rd Brigade was to take the Orchard and a locality which was called M10 but which was otherwise unidentified.

At 7.45 P.M., on the 20th, the 16th Battalion again went gallantly forward. Spread out at intervals of two paces, the Highlanders walked towards the enemy lines as coolly as though on manoeuvres. One soldier recorded the experience in his diary the next day: "The machine-gun fire was like sleet. Bill and I kept together at first. At the worst of the fire, Bill got scored over the forehead and turning to me said: 'Gee! Them bullets have the flies up north beat a mile.'"

Although the 16th Battalion suffered heavy losses, it reached the Orchard (hereafter throughout the war known as Canadian Orchard), cleared it, and dug some sort of trench line on the far side. M10, which turned out to be a fortified house surrounded by impassable belts of barbed wire, could not be approached, let alone taken. The 15th Battalion, horribly thinned by machine-gun fire, captured a German position known as the North Breastwork, but was halted a hundred yards beyond.

On the 2nd Brigade's front the attack was even less successful. Brigadier-General Currie, who had made a personal reconnaissance from the front line that afternoon, had been unable to identify the objective given to his 10th Battalion. It was marked on the map by the mystic symbol K5 surrounded by a circle, and nothing on the ground looked in the least like that. (It was, in fact, merely a narrow sector of the enemy line with no distinguishing feature of its own.) He had made a strong plea for the attack to be postponed. Not only had he been refused, but his fire support had actually been reduced. However, the Canadian men in the ranks were nothing if not willing. They had never been to war before and for all they knew this was the way things had to be. They felt that perhaps they were only pawns on a gigantic strategic chessboard, sacrificed reluctantly by the intelligence directing the game in order to ensure the success of some brilliant combination play elsewhere. The 10th Battalion struggled ahead about a hundred yards, losing men with every step, until the surviving company commanders called a halt to the suicidal business.

The Canadians were thrown in again the next day, at the same place and in the same senseless manner. The artillery preparation was utterly inadequate, both because there were not enough guns and because those that were allotted were short of ammunition. The enemy wire was not cut and the enemy machine guns were not silenced. The 10th Battalion, aided by the grenadiers of the 1st Brigade, moved off at 8.30 P.M., in the clear brightness of the May evening, well before twilight fell.

The left-hand company was cut to pieces almost as soon as the men jumped over the parapet, but the right-hand company reached the German front line and cleared a portion of it before being stopped. Several counterattacks were beaten off during the night, and thereafter the enemy merely turned his guns on the captured ground. Canadian casualties mounted so rapidly that Currie, on his own initiative, ordered the battalion to withdraw to its original position at noon the next day. This abortive operation cost the 10th Battalion 18 officers and 250 other ranks.

That was the situation which had called down Sir Douglas Haig's wrath on May 22 and which led to his ordering yet further attacks. He was particularly scathing about Currie's men being unable to capture K5. His sole concession to reality was that he dissolved "Alderson's Force" four days after he had created it. In the light of such evidence, it is difficult to understand how Haig's most recent biographer, John Terraine, can make on Haig's behalf the barefaced claim that "Whenever he did intervene [in his subordinates' conduct of operations] it was always on the side of reason and common sense." There was, unfortunately, little of either commodity noticeable at Festubert.

The next attack went in at 2.30 on the morning of May 24. The 5th Battalion took K5 and about 130 yards of trench running northwest from that strong-point. The assault cost the unit 13 of the 18 officers who participated and 237 other ranks.

Brigadier-General M. S. Mercer's 1st Brigade was then ordered to break out of the Orchard. Neither Mercer nor Lieutenant-Colonel R. Rennie, the commanding officer of the 3rd (Toronto) Battalion, designated as the assaulting unit, was enthusiastic over the task. They had both seen the ground.

Out in no-man's-land long-dead bodies festered alongside those of soldiers recently killed. Attempts to bury them had been abandoned because any sign of movement brought down a hail of whiz-bangs and machine-gun fire from the alert enemy. The whole area was as flat as the top of a table, without cover of any kind.

The Toronto men went over the top at 11.30 P.M., after an ineffective artillery bombardment lasting six hours had warned the Germans of exactly where the attack was coming. What everyone had dreaded immediately occurred. No sooner had the Canadians climbed the parapet and started across no-man's-land than they were met by the murderous enfilade fire of four machine guns on their right flank at distances of from 50 to 150 yards. Obviously, it would be insane to continue and Colonel Rennie called off the attack. Even so, the Toronto Regiment lost 8 officers and 158 men, most of them within a few seconds.

Even this was not the end of the Battle of Festubert. The high command was hard to convince. On the evening of May 25, "Seely's Detachment", another *ad hoc* group, consisting this time of nine squadrons of dismounted cavalry from the Royal Canadian Dragoons and Lord Strathcona's Horse, commanded by Brigadier-General the Right Honourable J. E. B. Seely, attempted to take the position enigmatically known as L8. Most of the cavalrymen had never been in the trenches before and the maps they were given were worse than useless. Working their way north from K5, they got hopelessly lost and occupied the wrong feature.

For the next two days there was some heated debate at divisional headquarters between Brigadier-General Mercer and General Alderson as to whether the Canadians should continue to carry out Haig's orders of the 22nd. At last the conclusion was reached that "the salient about the Orchard was not a suitable position from which to attack". That this was sound common sense is perhaps proved by the fact that the eastern end of Canadian Orchard remained the Allied front line until March 1918, when the Germans surged forward to capture all the ground that had been so bitterly contested in May 1915. The five separate Canadian attacks at Festubert had advanced the line an average of 600 yards along a mile of front, and for this the cost had been 2,468 casualties.

Although the purely tactical lessons of more than fifty

46

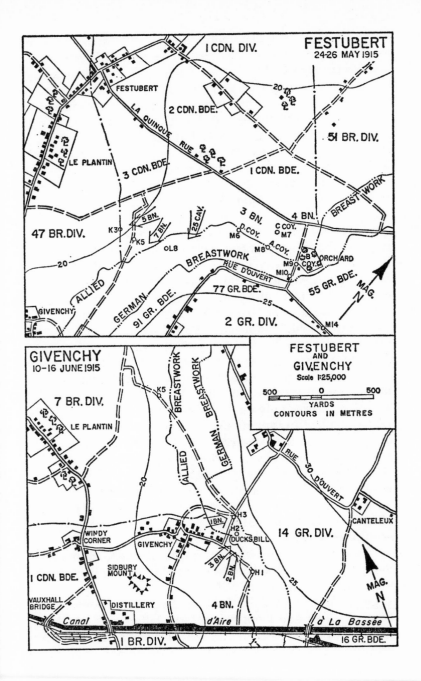

years ago can have little but historical interest now – since weapons systems have changed so greatly – there is surely something still to be learned from such engagements as Festubert. The area should not have been selected for an attack in the first place, but, even if there had been some overriding reason why the assault had to be launched there and nowhere else, the local commanders should at least have been allowed discretion as to the timing and nature of the attack. The fiction of omniscience maintained by First Army, and supported far too long by Corps and Division, was inevitably punished by failure. More pertinent than any purely tactical question, however, is the speculation as to whether there was not something radically wrong with the entire system of military command and control which could allow commanders so recklessly to waste human life. Discipline, which should be the formative, structural principle that shapes and quickens any body of fighting men – and which, in fact, was exactly this, and most splendidly, at the battalion level – was all too often at higher formations an obscurant that prevented the exposure of folly and the just punishment of stupidity. Haig, of course, was seriously culpable. But what are we to say of the military – and, ultimately, of the political – system that allowed an army commander to act thus with impunity? To lay the blame only on the incompetence of individuals is far too shallow an explanation. Nations, it is said, get the kind of government they deserve, but the dictum is even more immediately applicable to military command in war. Nothing exposes quite as ruthlessly as battle the respectable fictions, the polite lies, and the comfortable compromises of an unhealthy society. But before Britain is too much blamed for the social standards that made her peacetime army the preserve of privilege and the graveyard of ability, it would be well to remember that von Moltke was the German commander-in-chief at the outbreak of the war and that Sam Hughes was the Canadian Minister of Militia.

On the last day of May the Canadians moved south to the Givenchy area and went into reserve billets around Oblinghem, Essars, and Béthune. It was pleasant to be out of the line, to eat eggs and chips in the *estaminets*, and to drink the

Lunch time in the trenches, June 1916

The ruins of the cathedral at Ypres, Belgium, July 1916

In August 1916 General Sir Sam Hughes visited the Canadian troops in England and at the front. Here he is shown with a group of soldiers in training.

A soldier receiving first aid, August 1916

No-man's-land in front of the Canadian lines at Courcelette, October 1916

The famous "Hanging Virgin" at the cathedral at Albert, October 1916

Canadian troops returning from the trenches pass pack mules loaded with ammunition on their way to the guns, November 1916.

A Canadian soldier covered with mud returning from the front, March 1917

Canadian machine-gunners digging in during the advance on Vimy Ridge, April 1917

Men of the 17th Battalion C.F.A. firing a captured gun at the retreating Germans during the Battle of Vimy Ridge

A tank in action, July 1917

harsh *vin ordinaire* that was made palatable only by the addition of a little grenadine. The weather was warm and the soldiers enjoyed swimming naked in the La Bassée Canal, until some staff officer, shocked by the crowds of women who lined the canal banks to watch the men at their aquatic sports, forbade anyone to swim without "an adequate bathing costume". Since this was an item of equipment few soldiers thought to bring to France, the swimming came to a sudden end. However, some ingenious enthusiast hit on the idea of cutting two leg holes in a sandbag; modesty was saved and the men were able to enjoy their brief period of relaxation.

During the first ten days of June the Canadian Division was officially issued with Lee-Enfield rifles to replace the Ross, which had proved so treacherous a weapon at Second Ypres. Many soldiers had anticipated this order. After the fighting around St. Julien, 1,452 of the surviving Canadian infantrymen had thrown away their Rosses and picked up Lee-Enfields left on the field by dead or wounded Imperials.

The Canadian Division's new front, running from the La Bassée Canal to the village of Givenchy, was a narrow sector that required only one brigade in the line at a time. To everyone's delight the trenches here proved to be dry, even in the low ground near the canal, and unusually well constructed. No-man's-land was between 150 and 250 yards wide, except at a spot some 500 yards east of Givenchy where a semi-circular parapet of revetted sandbags, known as the Duck's Bill, protruded towards the enemy lines only 75 yards away. The heavily wired German positions had irregular parapets laid out with blue, red, purple, and white sandbags in broken patterns that made identification and range-finding difficult.

British engineers were hard at work digging a mine in the Canadian sector, a novelty that made the troops holding the front line somewhat nervous. What the British could do, the enemy could also do. It was disconcerting to come across sappers crouched in odd places with listening sets. Rat holes began to look suspicious, and more than one man reported that he heard strange noises underground. As well as the new hazard of mines, there was sporadic shelling and sniping, and since memories of the German gas attack at Ypres were

49

still fresh in everyone's mind, the weathercocks set up at battalion headquarters were watched with anxious eyes for any change in the wind.

The period of relative calm was not to last long. The French were about to renew their unsuccessful offensive against Vimy Ridge and again they called on the British for support. On June 15 the 1st (Ontario) Battalion was ordered to capture two German strong-points known as H2 and H3. The Canadians, who were learning rapidly, made every possible preparation with the resources available. Assembly and communication trenches were dug behind the front line; Brigadier-General H. E. Burstall, commander of the divisional artillery, insisted that the infantry express themselves satisfied with the wire-cutting program before the attack, and he had three 18-pounder guns moved secretly into the front line to give point-blank supporting fire; the 6th Battery, C.F.A., was hidden in a ruined farmhouse only 300 yards from H3; and a 3,000-pound mine was laid near H2.

At 5.45 P.M. on the 15th the field guns in the front line were unmasked and two of them began firing at the German front trench. The third gun was unable to open fire because it could not clear the parapet. The two 18-pounders were both knocked out of action by German shellfire, but not before they had placed 120 rounds exactly on target. However, the enemy's retaliatory shelling caused heavy casualties in the crowded assembly trenches.

H2 lay only seventy-five yards away, across from the Duck's Bill, but because of subterranean water the tunnel the engineers had dug did not quite reach the German position. The mine was blown promptly at 5.58 and a huge crater, forty feet across, was formed on the instant, but H2 itself was not damaged. Even worse, the explosion and the flying debris killed or wounded nearly fifty men of the 1st Battalion and detonated or buried most of the unit's bomb reserves.

This was an inauspicious beginning, but sharp at six o'clock the attacking troops walked forward past the writhing bodies of their own wounded who lay with broken backs and shattered limbs about the crater. At first the attack was successful. The first two waves reached the German second position, and although the third and fourth waves were badly thinned by machine-gun fire the 1st Battalion reported all four of its companies in the enemy lines by seven o'clock. The assaulting infantry carried blue flags to mark their progress and observers in the supporting battalion could see these moving forward above the top of the German trenches.

However, as the situation clarified, a less satisfactory picture of the evening's fighting gradually took shape. Neither British division attacking on the flanks had made appreciable progress; on the right the Highlanders of the 51st Division had been cut down in no-man's-land even before they reached the undamaged enemy wire. German machine guns swept the whole Canadian sector and by eight o'clock the only way to reach the 1st Battalion was along the collapsed mine gallery leading towards H2.

Enemy counterattacks slowly drove the 1st Battalion back along the trenches it had captured. The Canadians fought desperately, but their supply of bombs ran out, and the blue flags could now be seen retreating foot by foot. By ten o'clock the few survivors were back in their own trenches. In four hours the 1st Battalion had lost 20 officers and 346 other ranks.

At 10.30 that night the 3rd (Toronto) Battalion was ordered to renew the attack, but as word came in of the complete failure on both flanks this assault was postponed, first until 5.30 the next morning, and then indefinitely. In the remaining hours of darkness rescue parties brought in the wounded from no-man's-land and carried them out on stretchers to the long line of waiting ambulances. As soon as one of these was filled it lurched off to the dressing station at Bethune, where it was hurriedly unloaded and turned about again for another trip.

At noon the next day the Canadians were informed that they would have to try once more to take the same objectives. The new attack would have to be made without the careful preparations that had preceded the one on the 15th; this time there would be no mine to be exploded and no field guns in the front line; in fact, ammunition shortages meant that there could not even be an adequate artillery bombardment. By now, too, the enemy was fully alerted.

With the same insistence on daylight attacks, zero hour

was fixed for 4.45 on the afternoon of June 16. When the men of the 3rd Battalion leapt from their trenches they were at once met with a withering machine-gun fire that cut them down within feet of their own parapet. German infantrymen in the front trench picked off with rifles the odd Canadian who remained on his feet. An officer of the 2nd (East. Ontario) Battalion who witnessed the action reported: "This attack seemed, and seems, from every angle one viewed it, as futile and hopeless. . . . The attackers had no supporting fire. They were mostly shot down as they climbed over the parapets. None of them got over 25 yards, except perhaps a few who were trapped in the sap and could do nothing but lie low and await a chance to return."

Yet even this was not the end. At 5.30 the same afternoon the attack was renewed again, in exactly the same place, in exactly the same way, and with exactly the same result. It was then decided that the Royal Canadian Dragoons with infantry bombers attached, and supported by the 2nd and 3rd battalions, would assault over the identical ground at nine o'clock that evening. For some reason this attack was cancelled and the Battle of Givenchy came to an end.

The actions at Festubert and Givenchy were the first offensive operations in which the Canadians were engaged. They were relatively small affairs but in them there can already be discerned the pattern that was to endure for the next two and a half years. It was a pattern which, repeated on a larger scale, imposed itself on the Somme and Passchendaele. It came within a hair's-breadth of losing the war and the price it exacted in lives and morale had a deleterious effect that lasted for more than a generation. The basic fault is easy to detect: Allied commanders were more concerned with appearance than with reality. They were more worried about the moral effects of failure than about the decimation, and the more than decimation, of their own forces.

This, certainly, had not always been the British way of waging war. A hundred years previously the Duke of Wellington had said: "I knew that in my early years in the Peninsula, if I were to lose 500 men without the clearest necessity, I should be recalled and brought upon my knees to the bar of the House of Commons."

The change between Wellington's unwritten terms of reference and those of Sir John French and Sir Douglas Haig reflected an even deeper change in society as a whole. There was, in the first place, the especial *hubris* of the age. It had been this, more than any other thing, that had brought on the war itself. In the long and splendid autumn that was the end of the nineteenth century, and whose warm afterglow was still bright in August 1914, men had too confidently concerned themselves with abstractions. Poverty, hunger, and crime were "the economic problem"; violence, oppression, and exploitation were "imperial destiny"; and warfare was viewed through a romantic haze of glory. Hand in hand with this there was an unhealthy reverence for the omniscience of military authority, and a positively pathological belief in that omniscience by military authority itself. Apologists have written of the "determination" of men like Joffre, Foch, and Haig; but it seems at least possible that the quality they displayed was in reality the opposite of determination. There was something essentially brittle in so great a lack of flexibility, and the capacity for self-delusion that could sacrifice men by their tens of thousands rather than abandon a mental picture or fantasy was evidence of a lack of moral toughness. It was a refusal to face reality.

Towards the end of June the Canadian Division moved seventeen miles north of Givenchy to the Ploegsteert area. Here, for the remainder of the summer, the Canadians used the pick and shovel more than the rifle and grenade, for "Plugstreet" was delightfully quiet. Before long the Canadian trenches were models of their kind, nicely sandbagged and baked hard and brown by the sun. For the time being both sides practised a philosophy of live and let live. In the line the Canadians whiled away the long days cooking strange delicacies over little wood fires, and the reserve billets in the Piggeries, Bulford Camp, and Neuve Eglise were comfortable. There were still snipers, patrols, and the odd bit of shelling, but the locations about Plugstreet – Alderson's Avenue, Poole's Cottage, Kent House, and Grand Manque Farm – had few of the bitter memories associated with other sectors.

In July Sam Hughes inspected some Canadian units behind the front and no one was surprised to find that he had managed to get himself promoted to major-general. The Prime Minister, Sir Robert Borden, also visited the troops, as did the French minister of war, Millerand, Field Marshal Sir John French, and Lord Kitchener. The soldiers felt no great enthusiasm for such visits. Although an inspection by the mighty ones ensured a few days of safety out of the line, it meant long hours of preparatory spit and polish, a period of seemingly interminable waiting, and very often having to listen to a ludicrously patriotic speech.

In September the 2nd Canadian Division arrived in France and the Canadian Corps was formed. General Alderson became corps commander; Arthur Currie was promoted to command the 1st Division; and R. E. W. Turner was given command of the 2nd Division. This arrangement satisfied everyone, except perhaps Sam Hughes who had toyed with the splendid possibility of retaining his appointment of Minister of Militia while commanding the Canadian Corps in person. During four years of war the Canadians were spared little, but this at least was one horror that passed them by. At the end of September the strength of the Canadian Corps stood at 1,354 officers and 36,522 other ranks.

The period of relative comfort ended abruptly in the last week of October when the autumn rains began. Day after day the skies opened and the rain poured down. The front line provided no refuge from the universal wetness, and men spent their entire tour of duty soaked to the skin, without rubber boots or effective raincapes. The trenches, of which the Canadians had been so proud, literally began to ooze away as the sun-baked clay dissolved and the fillings of sandbags trickled out in liquid mud. Dugouts collapsed; parapets, parados, and revetments caved in; and the Germans, who, as always, were on somewhat higher ground, happily drained their trenches over no-man's-land. Out of the line, conditions were little better: the hutments leaked, the charcoal fires smoked furiously but gave little heat, and everyone was wet, cold, and miserable.

As 1915 drew to a close little comfort could be taken from the Allies' military situation. After the British had fought another disastrous battle at Loos, Sir John French had been replaced as commander-in-chief by Sir Douglas Haig. Turkey had entered the war on Germany's side, and on the Eastern Front Russia had suffered a succession of paralysing defeats. A clumsily executed British expedition to the Dardanelles had failed bloodily on the beaches of Cape Hellas and the shores of Sulva Bay.* A Franco-British force had been bottled up in Salonika, and a British expedition under General Sir Charles Townshend was surrounded at Kut in Mesopotamia.

At the end of 1915 on the Western Front British forces, including the Canadians, totalled 987,000, as compared with 2,752,000 French and some 2,800,000 Germans. The Germans, in fact, were outnumbered in the west by 150 divisions to 125 and on the Eastern Front by 141 divisions to 90, while in the whole global war the Allies had a superiority of more than 100 divisions over the Central Powers. Nevertheless, the enemy had definitely had the better of the fighting. This was certainly not because the individual German soldier was tougher, braver, or more skilful than his opponent, or because the German regimental officers were better at their job. Yet if the British, French, and Russians suffered from all the disadvantages inherent in an alliance, so did the Germans and Austrians. Political ineptitude was about the same on both sides at this stage of the war, and although Germany's central position and her wonderful east-west transportation system were certainly great assets, they were more than offset by the Allied control of the seas.

The truth was that for at least the first three years of the war the German armies were consistently better led and more ably handled at the army and army group level than those of the Allies. It may come as a shock to those brought up on legends of rigid Prussian militarism, but one reason – and probably the principal one – for the more able German control of operations was that the German system of command was very much more flexible than the British. Senior German commanders and their staffs were far readier to listen to the arguments of their front-line subordinates and were much more willing to modify their preconceived ideas of what was

* The Newfoundland Regiment had participated in this campaign as part of the 29th British Division.

tactically feasible. The Germans, moreover, possessed a much sounder corpus of operational doctrine. Such subtle concepts as that of *Schwerpunkt* – that an attack should have a "centre of gravity" – were undreamt of at British G.H.Q. General Max Hoffmann, a brilliant German staff officer on the Eastern Front, summed it up well. When one of his colleagues remarked admiringly that British troops fought like lions, Hoffmann fixed his monocle in his eye, smiled his schoolboyish smile, and replied: "Yes. Isn't it fortunate that they are led by donkeys?"

On February 21, 1916, the Germans suddenly attacked at Verdun, thereby upsetting the Allied plans for the year and beginning the first of the murderous battles of attrition that were eventually to exhaust all the belligerents. Although it was not entirely apparent at the time, the battle of Verdun was the second serious German mistake of the war, the first having been the modification of the Schlieffen Plan in 1914. If Falkenhayn had been content to remain on the defensive in the west in 1916, letting the British and French break their teeth against his lines, and had instead made his major effort against the Russians in the east, the war might have ended very differently. Once again it is interesting to note that the Germans, who were so good at the tactical and operational levels, were often surprisingly inept strategically.

No Canadian, of course, in the army or in the government, could take more than an academic interest in this type of problem. The 3rd Canadian Division had been formed in December under Major-General M. S. Mercer, the former commander of the 1st Brigade. Princess Patricia's Canadian Light Infantry, which had served for a year with the British 27th Division, now joined the 3rd Division, as did the Royal Canadian Regiment, which had done garrison duty in Bermuda. On April 1 the Canadian Corps returned to the Ypres Salient to take over a stretch of line running from the vicinity of St. Eloi to near Hooge on the Menin Road. As the infantry trudged up to the front they wore for the first time the round, basin-like steel helmets that had just been issued on a scale of fifty per company.

The new sector was not a healthy one. Four days previously the British had blown six huge mines beneath the German line at St. Eloi. The earth had trembled for miles around and the noise of the explosions had been heard as far away as Folkestone in Kent. Before the debris had finished falling, the 3rd British Division had advanced to occupy the craters and the shattered German front line. By error the British had seized only five of the seven great holes in the ground – one crater had already been in existence before March 27 – but after severe fighting they had won possession of the other two.

When the Canadian Corps took over the sector from the V British Corps on April 4, a front line simply did not exist. The entire battlefield was water-logged; shell holes and mine craters were ponds; and the so-called trench system was no more than a series of drainage ditches. The 2nd Division's 6th Brigade, commanded by Brigadier-General H. D. B. Ketchen, manned the line with the 27th (City of Winnipeg) Battalion on the right and the 31st (Alberta) Battalion on the left. There was a gap between the two battalions, and the Canadian positions were under constant observed artillery fire from the Germans on Wytschaele Ridge. What a Canadian could see of the battlefield was limited to what was visible at ground level – and, for those who have not tried since childhood to look at the world from this vantage point, this means that Canadian fields of observation were very seriously limited. The Canadian front was devoid of wire; no one knew for sure where the enemy was, or even where other Canadian positions were located; and all the craters looked maddeningly identical. The 27th Battalion's position could be reached only by circuitous routes around either flank, for the ground between the mine craters in the centre was impassable. During their first two days in the line the men suffered heavily from German shelling, sleep was impossible, and the constant artillery fire, combined with exhaustion, resulted in a number of cases of shell shock. At 3.30 on the raw, wet morning of April 6, while the 29th (Vancouver) Battalion was relieving the 27th, a German attack won back all the ground that had been gained since March 27.

A series of local Canadian counterattacks failed, and when the 31st (Alberta) Battalion tried to retake Craters 4 and 5 it mistakenly occupied Craters 6 and 7. No one on the staff detected the error in spite of the fact that aerial photographs taken on April 8 provided a sure means of identifying the craters that had been occupied. This error was not discovered for ten days. On the night of April 6–7, the 4th Brigade relieved the 6th Brigade, which had lost 617 men in four days. Still no one really knew where the German positions were or which craters were which. A night attack launched by the 21st (Eastern Ontario) Battalion on April 8–9 was beaten back, and a three-battalion attack the next night by the 18th (Western Ontario), 20th (Central Ontario), and 21st battalions suffered the same fate.

On the 16th, after a belated examination of aerial photographs, General Turner and his divisional staff were sadly shocked to learn that the Germans, not the Canadians, actually held the craters. By now the Canadians had lost 1,373 men at St. Eloi, compared to a German loss of 483, and the enemy was still in possession of the disputed area. The news was unwelcome at Corps and Army as well, and General Plumer, the able commander of Second British Army, wanted to remove both Turner and Ketchen from their commands. Haig, however, decided otherwise. He had heard that there was "some feeling against the English" among Canadian troops, and he feared that the removal of two Canadian senior officers might start "a serious feud between the Canadians and the British". The next month, as a result of the bad feeling generated by the failure at St. Eloi, General Alderson was replaced as commander of the Canadian Corps by General Sir Julian Byng, a British cavalry officer who had commanded a corps at the Dardanelles and on the Western Front.

Although May was officially a "quiet" month for the Canadian Corps, 2,000 Canadians were killed or wounded in the Salient. The casualties were part of the normal "wastage" suffered in holding that particular piece of ground. Men would be hit in communications trenches, even when they obeyed the grimly humorous signs which exhorted them: "Keep your head down. Your King and Country need you." They would be hit at night while on working parties or while they slept under inadequate cover. And always, day or night, the stray artillery shell might streak through the sky like a long, impersonal talon to claim its prey.

While the 2nd Division stayed on at St. Eloi, the 1st Division held the line about the Hill 70 area, and Major-General Mercer's 3rd Division, with four battalions up, garrisoned the most easterly portion of the Salient. In this area north of Hill 70 was Mount Sorrel and Observatory Ridge, running west from a hill called Tor Top towards Armagh Wood and Sanctuary Wood. Behind these, in the direction of Ypres, a shallow valley contained the ruined village of Zillebeke and the stagnant pond known as Zillebeke Lake. The Canadian line ran through Mount Sorrel, Hill 61, and Tor Top.

On the night of May 31 the units of Brigadier-General V. A. S. Williams' 8th Brigade arrived in Ypres from divisional reserve. They marched up past Shrapnel Corner, Railway Dugouts, and Transport Farm, where guides from the 9th Brigade met them and led them forward to the line. Only the occasional gun-flash and flare split the darkness. The 4th Canadian Mounted Rifles took up positions on Mount Sorrel, and the 1st C.M.R. moved into trenches on Observatory Ridge. June 1 passed uneventfully, and at eight o'clock the next morning Major-General Mercer and Brigadier-General Williams arrived at the 4th C.M.R.'s battalion headquarters to inspect Tor Top and Mount Sorrel.

The June day was warm and clear, the Salient was quiet, and high in the central blue of the sky larks sang as though there was no war below. Suddenly out of that quiet sky every German gun about the Salient poured shells upon the 8th Brigade's line. The bombardment far exceeded anything so far seen on the Western Front. Sanctuary Wood, Armagh Wood, and Maple Copse were torn to tatters, trenches simply disappeared, dugouts fell in, and the weed-covered ground was turned over as though by some monstrous plough. For four hours the enemy artillery blasted the Canadian line from half a mile west of Mount Sorrel to the northern edge of Sanctuary Wood.

In Armagh Wood General Mercer had his eardrums ruptured and his leg broken by a shell burst, and as he lay helpless on the ground he was killed by shrapnel. Brigadier-General Williams was seriously wounded and subsequently captured by the enemy. At one o'clock the bombardment stopped as suddenly as it had begun. The pause was only momentary. Seconds later the ground quivered and heaved; there came the roar of four mines being exploded; and sandbags, wire, machine guns, and bodies were hurled upwards from the 4th C.M.R. position.

Then the German infantry appeared in the bright afternoon sunlight. They swarmed over the battered ground, coming forward confidently and at a leisurely pace, long spades slung over their shoulders. No one was left to resist them. Of the 22 officers and 680 men of the 4th C.M.R.s who had come into the line thirty-six hours before only 3 officers and 73 men survived. The unit had suffered casualties amounting to 89 per cent of its strength. The German infantry – they were Württembergers of the 26th and 27th Infantry divisions – flowed over Mount Sorrel and Tor Top. On the flanks of the attack Princess Patricia's Canadian Light Infantry and the 5th Battalion fired into the enemy but could not stem the advance.

Moving along Observatory Ridge, the Germans came on two 18-pounder guns of the 5th Battery, C.F.A. The Canadian gunners loaded and fired over open sights until the barrels could be depressed no more, then fought on with their small arms until overrun. This was the only time in the war when Canadian guns, which are the artillery's colours, ever fell into enemy hands. The Germans gave full credit to the gallant defenders. One of their regimental historians later wrote: "It is fitting to stress that here too the Canadians did not surrender but defended themselves at their guns with revolvers to the last man." The Canadians recaptured these two guns later in the month.

The Germans swarmed into most of Armagh Wood, although Princess Patricia's Canadian Light Infantry checked the right wing of their advance. One Patricia company, even though all its officers were killed or wounded, fought on behind the German right rear for eighteen hours. On this day the Patricias lost 400 men, of whom 150, including the commanding officer, were killed.

By evening Canadian reserves had been rushed to the front and a new line established, but a local counterattack by four battalions was unsuccessful. Only the 49th (Edmonton) Battalion on the left regained a little of the lost ground.

Before a set-piece counterattack could be mounted, the Germans struck again, this time in the direction of Hooge. At 3.05 in the afternoon of June 6, after four more mines had been exploded, the Württembergers poured into the 28th (North-West) Battalion positions. They were halted before they reached the support trenches, but the situation looked increasingly ugly.

Haig, preparing for a major offensive on the Somme, was reluctant to allot additional infantry for a counterattack in the Salient, but the Canadians were given 218 guns. Because of the heavy casualties already suffered – the 7th Brigade had lost 1,050 men by June 4 – two composite brigade groups were formed. The 1st, 3rd, 7th, and 8th battalions were placed under Brigadier-General L. J. Lipsett for the counterattack on the right to retake Mount Sorrel, and the 2nd, 4th, 13th, and 16th battalions were grouped under Brigadier-General G. S. Tuxford to recapture Tor Top. The 58th Battalion and one company of the 52nd (Lake Superior) Battalion were to assault on the extreme left. Vile weather with high winds and almost continuous rain postponed the attack, but the massed guns softened up the enemy between June 9 and June 12. At 1.30 in the morning of the 13th, in heavy rain and under cover of a dense smoke screen, the Canadian infantry went over the top with the 3rd, 16th, 13th, and 58th battalions leading the assault.

The night was dark and the going rough. For most units the way led uphill, through thick mud, over ground gaping with water-filled shell holes, and around broken clumps of enemy wire, shattered trees, and patches of tangled undergrowth. The rain drizzled down from a starless sky, and all that could be seen ahead was the orange splash of bursting shells and the intermittent, firefly twinkle of German rifle fire. The noise of the bombardment was so loud that a man could shout at the top of his lungs to a comrade only a foot away and not be heard.

Here and there gaps appeared in the advancing Canadian lines, but platoons and sections closed instinctively on the dimly seen figure of some officer or N.C.O. and pushed on. The attack was completely successful. Almost 200 prisoners were taken, and by 2.30 the 3rd (Toronto) Battalion was in possession of Mount Sorrel, the 16th (Canadian Scottish) Battalion had retaken the northern portion of Armagh Wood, the 13th Battalion (Royal Highlanders of Canada) was firmly on Observatory Ridge and Tor Top, and the 58th Battalion had recaptured the former Canadian line running through Sanctuary Wood. In the grey, rainy dawn, enemy counterattacks were broken up by artillery fire.

The battle was over, and the Canadians had won their first clear-cut victory of the war. It had, it is true, been an expensive victory. Casualties had been heavy – between June 2 and June 14 the corps lost some 9,600 men as compared to German casualties of 5,765 – but a high proportion of the Canadian casualties had been suffered before the final, successful assault. And although the ground itself was not worth the price paid for it the attack was certainly justified because of its effect on morale, a consideration especially important after the recent fiasco among the craters of St. Eloi.

At Mount Sorrel the key to success had been meticulous

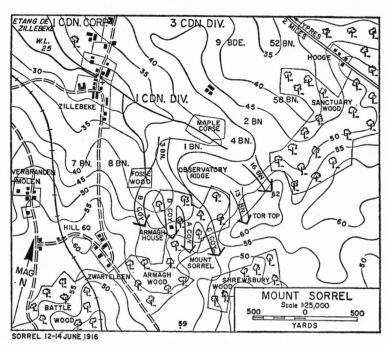

SORREL 12-14 JUNE 1916

preparation and intelligent planning. Unlike Festubert, this attack had been launched under cover of darkness and smoke had been used further to blind and confuse the enemy. The problems of administration and supply had been worked out in detail, and careful registration had ensured the accuracy of the supporting artillery fire. Yet none of these factors would have given victory had it not been for the fine fighting spirit of the assaulting battalions. The soldiers themselves knew this, and they knew too that, if only the staff work was competent, they could capture any reasonable objective. By now they were no longer green troops but veterans.

The Canadians spent the rest of the summer in the Salient but were not committed to any major action. In mid August a 4th Division, under Major-General David Watson, took its place in the corps. By then everyone was watching with intense interest the progress of Haig's great offensive on the Somme.

All day columns of Canadian troops had marched over the crest of the ridge of hills that formed an amphitheatre around the little town of Albert in Picardy. As each file of fours reached the hilltop, the soldiers eagerly gazed down and saw, spread out below them like a panorama, the battlefield of the Somme. They had waited weeks for this moment, as though for the revelation of a mystery. Each man, as he stared, wondered what tomorrow would hold for him in the strange country down below. There was nothing particularly sinister about the line of sausage balloons hanging suspended along the front like toys at a fair, but the entire northeastern sky was lit by a flickering light and the deep rumble of guns ringed half the horizon.

The Battle of the Somme had already been raging furiously for two months, and every Canadian private knew that it was the greatest British offensive of the war, "the Big Push" by which the commander-in-chief, Sir Douglas Haig, intended to break through the German lines to final victory. However, no one was quite sure how it was going. The English newspapers were still enthusiastic, and "Comic Cuts", as the corps intelligence summaries were irreverently known, were professionally optimistic; but rumours of another sort had also been heard, even as far away as St. Omer where the Canadians had been training for their part in the battle. Partly owing to the unparalleled size of the operation and partly because the British government exercised little effective control over the employment of its field armies, a true picture was long in emerging. Now, on the last day of August 1916, the 1st, 2nd, and 3rd divisions of Sir Julian Byng's Canadian Corps – some 59,000 men in all – were completing their concentration on the Somme. For the time being the newly arrived 4th Division remained in the Ypres Salient to complete its training.

What the soldiers saw from the ridge above Albert was an array of ammunition dumps, engineer stores, hospitals, gun lines, cavalry encampments, and infantry bivouacs vaster and more imposing than anything they had imagined possible. Below them, in a few square miles, the entire strength of the British nation and Empire seemed to be concentrated for one supreme effort – as indeed it was.

Since the morning of July 1, when the battle had opened, this formerly insignificant corner of rural France had become a crucible of nations. Every minor landmark was already bitterly imprinted on the memory of a generation. The Canadians did not yet know it, but they were looking down on a scene of agony and death unprecedented in history. Beyond the white chalk scar of the old front line – only a little distance beyond – were the bloodstained ruins of the Sugar Factory, Pozières, Beaumont Hamel, Thiepval, Contalmaison, Delville Wood, and Mouquet Farm. Division after division of khaki-clad men had already marched down the straight poplar-lined stretch of the Route Nationale that ran from Amiens through Albert to Bapaume. But Bapaume still lay well behind the German lines, and tens of thousands who went up that road were never to return.

The decision to launch the Somme offensive had been taken in December 1915, at Chantilly, the headquarters of General Joffre, the French commander-in-chief. Haig and Joffre had decided it between them. The French and British would surge forward together, break the enemy lines, win the war, and silence forever those irritating "amateurs" who wanted to defeat Germany elsewhere than on the Western Front. However, the Germans had struck first, at Verdun, and pressed the French so hard that Haig had had to attack before he wished. Moreover, the frontage of assault had been drastically shortened and the attacking force reduced.

No strategic considerations had dictated that the attack be made astride the Somme River. No great prize lay behind the German front – no vital rail centre or industrial complex. The Germans could safely retire for miles, falling back on stronger positions to a shorter line, and, in fact, they did so in 1917. The point of attack had been chosen simply because it was here that the British and French sectors happened to join. Nor had any account been taken of the fact that the enemy defences on the Somme were the strongest on the entire Western Front. For eighteen quiet months the industrious Germans had been digging in the chalk hills above the Allied line. The result was an elaborate system of three trench lines, each protected by two belts of thick barbed wire thirty yards wide. For protection against Allied shelling there were spacious dugouts, thirty and sometimes forty feet deep, comfortably furnished with bunks, tables, and armchairs, carpeted, ventilated, and lit by electricity. The Germans lived well inside them, and Canadian soldiers were later to be amazed at the stores of cigars, brandy, tinned meats, and bottled beer they discovered in these strongholds. Concrete and sandbagged fortresses on the spurs of the hillsides provided deadly enfilade fire across much of the front.

Undismayed by any of this, Haig began his preparations months ahead of time, with an almost complete disregard for secrecy. The Big Push was common gossip in France and England. A British cabinet minister, in an incautious speech to munitions workers, had even indicated the approximate date of the attack. Day by day along the Somme the ammunition and stores dumps grew, railway lines were extended, aerodromes were built, batteries moved in, and three-quarters of a million men, in twenty-nine British and eight French divisions, gathered for the battle. In G.H.Q. reserve, close behind the front, Haig massed five cavalry divisions whose task it would be to exploit the breakthrough in the open country far to the enemy's rear. At first the Germans watched these preparations incredulously, then with a sort of amazed belief. They took what countermeasures seemed necessary, but when the battle opened they had only eight and two-thirds divisions deployed along the frontage of attack.

Before the battle Haig moved his headquarters nearer the

front to the gracious grey-stone Château de Valvion at Beauquesne, twelve miles behind the line. Psychologically he was still as far away from the realities of the battle area as he would have been in a spacecraft orbiting the moon. Every morning before breakfast he walked in the château garden and every afternoon he went horseback riding, escorted by his private guard from the 17th Lancers. As the fateful day drew near he confided to his diary: "I feel that every step in my plan has been taken with the Divine help."

The British artillery roared continuously for seven days before the attack, but with a neat impartiality distributed its fire equally over the front rather than concentrating on strong-points. Although most of the guns were of light or medium calibre and some of the ammunition was defective, the earth-shaking thunder they produced was impressive. General Sir Henry Rawlinson, commander of the Fourth Army, assured his subordinates that "nothing could exist at the conclusion of the bombardment in the area covered by it"; the infantry would merely walk over and occupy the pulverized enemy positions. The soldiers massed in the rear areas believed it, for they had never heard so tremendous a bombardment before, but the battalions and brigades holding the line often reported apprehensively that the German wire in front of them was uncut. These reports were generally ignored.

At 7.30 on the morning of July 1 the guns suddenly ceased firing. Along the eighteen miles of British front whistles blew, officers waved their men forward, and a hundred thousand volunteers of Kitchener's New Army went over the top into the tall grass of no-man's-land where wild mustard, blue cornflowers, and red poppies grew. It was three hours after dawn and a lovely summer's day. Since each of the attacking soldiers was burdened down with sixty-six pounds of ammunition, rations, entrenching tools, and equipment, the long lines advanced at a slow walk. This point is worth reflection. The staff decreed that these troops should be sent to fight the greatest battle of Britain's history under the handicap of a load-to-weight ratio considerably in excess of the maximum load-to-weight ratio permissible for pack mules. They sent them, so laden, across open fields by broad daylight against uncut wire. The staff had decreed it and the commanders had concurred.

As soon as the British bombardment lifted, the Germans came out of their dugouts to man their parapets. In some cases the peculiar stuttering rattle of their machine guns began before the first wave of attackers was clear of the front trench. The British fell in their thousands. Some toppled back into their own trenches; some went down halfway across no-man's-land; some reached the German wire and raged helplessly there until death stilled them. A very few worked their way forward to the enemy first line to fight an impossible battle until driven back or slaughtered. It was Festubert and Givenchy all over again, on a greater scale but for the same reasons.

The Newfoundland Regiment, belonging to the British 29th Division, was virtually annihilated in front of the little village of Beaumont Hamel. The Newfoundlanders started out from a support position, and enemy shells were falling among them even before they crossed their own front trenches. As they threaded their way through the sally ports in their own wire, machine-gun fire cut them down, but the survivors, stepping over the wounded and dying, pushed determinedly on. Only a handful reached the German wire and these were killed or captured there. In less than half an hour the Newfoundland Regiment lost every one of the 26 officers who took part in the attack and 674 other ranks. Each year on Commemoration Day, which is fixed by statute as the Sunday nearest July 1, almost every family in Newfoundland still mourns some loved one who fell at Beaumont Hamel.

Immediately north of the Somme the XIII British Corps captured Montauban under cover of the first creeping barrage of the war, and the XV British Corps took the village of Mametz. Elsewhere the attack failed completely – in some sectors the Germans had not even bothered to call up their reserve battalions – and nightfall saw the shattered British divisions trying to evacuate their wounded from their own front line. The day's fighting had cost 57,470 casualties, of which nearly 20,000 were fatalities – by far the heaviest loss in the entire history of British arms.

South of the British sector, where General Fayolle's French

Sixth Army had attacked on a six-mile front with five divisions, the fortunes of the day were very different. A ground mist and better artillery preparation, combined with more flexible tactics, enabled the French to capture all their objectives north of the Somme before midday. South of the river the French had advanced about half a mile past their objective by evening. This success did not continue, and after the first day the French, like the British, settled down to a battle of attrition, although on a much smaller scale.

Haig gave no evidence of being disconcerted by the events of July 1. His plan, after all, was God's as well as his. On the 2nd, he ordered the attack renewed. That he was able to do so after the bloodiest defeat in British history, a defeat which had been brought about entirely by his own and his staff's incompetence, is a bitter comment on the inability of a nation to control its destiny in a major war.

For the next ten days the British lost some ten thousand men a day for negligible gains. In the middle of the month a night assault against Bazentin Ridge succeeded without excessive casualties and on the 23rd the Australians captured the village of Pozières after bloody fighting. This was hailed as a great victory and the Australians were very rightly praised for their courage and dash. Haig, however, had reservations. Towards the end of the month he wrote in his diary: "Some of their [the Australians'] Divisional Generals are so ignorant (and like many Colonials) so conceited, that they cannot even be trusted to work out unaided the plan of attack." This from the man who, so short a time before, had witlessly sacrificed nearly 60,000 men by a plan of attack as stupid as any in warfare!

August saw no change in the character of the battle. Both sides brought up reinforcements and committed divisions for the second, and sometimes for the third, time. In Britain, Lloyd George, Winston Churchill, and some other members of the cabinet were appalled by the terrible casualties; but strict censorship and misleading reports by staff officers who had never been to the front concealed the horrible truth from the British public.

When the Canadians arrived on the Somme at the end of August most of the German second line had been captured, but the third line remained intact and the enemy was busy building a fourth line behind it. Many Canadian units bivouacked in the Brickfields, a barren waste of chalky ground thinly covered with grass on a low ridge west of Albert. When it rained the Brickfields were inches deep in water, and the troops often sought shelter in the abandoned, roofless houses of the town, preferring shellfire to the misery of sleeping in the wet. On their way through the shattered streets they looked curiously at the famous "Hanging Virgin", the beautiful bronze image of the Blessed Mother with her Child that hung forward at a grotesque right-angle from the shell-damaged campanile of the Church of Notre Dame de Brebières. Superstition had it that when the pendant statue fell the war would end.

On August 31 Major-General Arthur Currie's 1st Division began relieving the Australians about Pozières. The Canadians moved up to the line through Sausage Valley, a desolate, shapeless depression between bare, pockmarked hills that the gunners had taken over as their own. Guns of all calibres were lined up in Sausage Valley almost wheel to wheel; the air was thick with cordite fumes; half-naked gunners toiled in the murk amid great piles of brass cartridge cases; and the noise of the firing was nerve-wracking. At the front the Canadians found the ground littered with the corpses of German and Australian dead, their discoloured, yellow faces and blackened mouths half-hidden by swarms of flies.

On September 3 the Australians tried for the sixth time to capture Mouquet Farm, and two companies of the 13th Battalion (Royal Highlanders of Canada) attacked with them. The farm was not taken, but some 300 yards of a German trench called Fabeck Graben were occupied. In this minor action the Royal Highlanders of Canada suffered 322 casualties, and in its first five days in the line the 3rd Brigade lost 970 men. On the 8th the Germans recaptured Fabeck Graben.

On September 5 Generals Hindenburg and Ludendorff, the brilliant team who had replaced General Falkenhayn in the German supreme command six days previously, assumed control of the Western Front. On the 6th they decided to evacuate the entire area between Soissons and Arras as soon as a strong new line had been built twenty miles to the rear.

The Canadians now found themselves fighting a terrible kind of war. Battalions would march up to the line over heavily shelled roads, always losing some men on the way. They would wait for days in shelled trenches before making another desperate advance that could be measured in yards. The new position, which looked exactly like the old, would either be held with loss or abandoned with still heavier loss. Then they would march back under shellfire for a day or two in rest billets before the cycle began again.

Under the ceaseless pounding of the guns the Somme battlefield had taken on a lunar aspect. Woods and coppices were no more than a few charred and smouldering sticks. Villages were only rubble heaps. Some, like Contalmaison, were indistinguishable from the churned-up ground around them, and only a painted signboard, erected by the provost corps, gave any indication of what had once been there. The debris of battle was everywhere – bits of bloodstained equipment, old tin cans, broken rifles, wire, rotting bodies, steel helmets, unexploded bombs. Smoke and gases polluted the atmosphere, and in the miserable holes that went by the name of dugouts the air was so bad that candles burned with only a feeble glimmer.

Only in the skies was there any clear evidence of Allied superiority. The Nieuport and Spad biplanes the British flew could definitely outmanoeuvre the German Fokker monoplanes. However, this domination of the air did not appreciably help those on the ground. By now the autumn was drawing in and there was as yet little to show for the bloodiest two and a half months' fighting in history. No strategic advantage had been won; the gain in ground was worthless; and the best of a generation had died. With them had died, too, much of Britain's hope for the future. The pressure on Verdun had been relieved, but Hindenburg and Ludendorff would certainly have halted the attacks at Verdun in any case. They had never agreed with Falkenhayn's plans for that battle. In Britain, where the truth could no longer be entirely concealed when the hospitals were filled with disillusioned wounded, there was mounting criticism of the continuing Somme offensive.

Sir Douglas Haig decided to launch another major attack in the hope of achieving the breakthrough that had so long eluded him. Again he optimistically massed five cavalry divisions behind the front to exploit the gap. Moreover, he decided to use a new secret weapon, the tank, although it was still in the developmental stage and only inadequate numbers were available.

In spite of the indifference of the War Office and the generals, the tank had been developed on the initiative of Winston Churchill when he had been First Lord of the Admiralty. Secret trials had been successful and a hundred machines had been ordered. The first tanks were slow, cumbersome, and subject to mechanical failure, but they could move over broken ground at nearly four miles an hour, cross ten-foot trenches, and crush barbed wire. Most important of all, they protected their crews from small-arms fire and shrapnel. The answer to the machine gun's domination of the battlefield thus proved to be a startlingly simple one – interpose half an inch of armour plate between the advancing attacker and the machine gun's stream of bullets. Employed in sufficient numbers and as a tactical surprise, the tanks could almost certainly have broken the trench deadlock and brought decisive victory. Nevertheless, against the advice of the technical experts and over the protests of Lloyd George and Churchill, Haig threw thirty-two tanks into battle in mid September, distributing them in small numbers over the frontage of attack. "And so," Lloyd George later wrote, "the great secret was sold for the battered ruin of a little hamlet."

It has been suggested that Haig, sensing that his own position as commander-in-chief had been weakened by the failure of the Somme offensive, threw in his handful of tanks as a last desperate gamble. Haig's biographer, John Terraine, has recently replied that Haig's action cannot possibly be termed a gamble because he had been considering using tanks on the Somme for five months before he actually did so. Whatever may have been Haig's motivation, the decision was certainly wrong. And is the man who ponders long before staking his fortune at the casino less a gambler than he who plunges spontaneously? A gamble is determined by the amount of risk involved, not by the length of the prior period of consideration.

At all events, the new attack began on September 15 with Rawlinson's Fourth Army and Gough's Reserve Army. The Canadian Corps was to assault on a 2,200-yard front and capture Candy Trench, the Sugar Factory, and 1,500 yards of Sugar Trench in front of the village of Courcelette. Major-General Turner's 2nd Division was to conduct the attack, while Major-General Lipsett's 3rd Division provided left-flank protection. Turner received all seven tanks allotted to the Canadians.

The 15th was a day of clear autumn weather, but at 6.20 in the morning, when the Canadians advanced behind a creeping barrage, there was a helpful mist in the hollows and on the slopes of hills. Aided by the tanks, which frequently threw the enemy into complete confusion, the attack went well. By eight o'clock all objectives had been reached and the sole remaining tank, whose nickname, Crème de Menthe, was chalked on its side, clanked back triumphantly to the Sugar Factory.

In the early evening the 4th and 6th brigades pushed on into Courcelette itself. The 22nd (French-Canadian) Battalion and the 25th Battalion (Nova Scotia Rifles) attacked with the bayonet and cleared the village after ten minutes' vicious hand-to-hand fighting. The French Canadians caught the defenders in the confusion of a relief and went through them like wolves through sheep. The portion of the village captured by the 22nd Battalion was turned into a bloody shambles. Dead and dying Germans lay everywhere about the ruined streets, and the whimpering and groaning of the wounded could be heard all night long. The commanding officer of the 22nd Battalion noted in his diary: "If hell is as bad as what I have seen in Courcelette, I would not wish my worst enemy to go there." The position was consolidated in the face of repeated, fierce counterattacks. By the time the Canadians left the line, the week's fighting had cost them 7,230 casualties. The main objectives, however, were not taken; the longed-for breakthrough was as far away as ever. What had actually been achieved was an advance of about one mile on a six-mile front. The cavalry, having had no chance to use their lances and sabres, moved back again.

A few hundred yards beyond the smoking ruins of Courcelette the battered earth sloped gently upward to form Thiepval Ridge. On this feature was Mouquet Farm, where so many Australians had died, Zollern Graben, Stuff Redoubt, Hessian Trench, and Regina Trench. Two entire corps, the Canadian and the 2nd British, were assigned the task of taking Thiepval Ridge, but it was to be a month before the little hill was finally cleared of the enemy.

In October the rains came. Soon the trenches were thigh-deep in yellow, slippery mud; it became an athletic feat to hoist oneself over the slimy parapets; the mud clung to boots and made walking a torture. Many wounded men slipped into water-filled shell holes or mud-filled trenches to drown or suffocate; perhaps most of those listed as missing at the Somme perished this way. Walking wounded took four hours to cover the two miles between their regimental aid post and the dressing station of Pozières.

Strict orders were issued against fraternization, but in spite of this Canadian and German stretcher-bearers sometimes met in no-man's-land around Kenora and Regina trenches and worked together side by side at similar tasks. Canadian wounded were sometimes dressed by German stretcher-bearers, and occasionally wounded prisoners were exchanged in no-man's-land. At a dressing station at Courcelette two captured German doctors tended Canadian wounded under shellfire for many hours. One of them objected to having a sentry stationed near his dugout, saying: "Your wounded are the same to me as ours." By now most front-line soldiers had little hatred left for the enemy they fought so savagely; the causes of the war and the war aims of the statesmen alike seemed to belong to another world.

Nevertheless, the battering-ram attacks went on day by day, as senior headquarters urged that "no opportunity for gaining ground be lost". The agonized British armies, heads down like wounded bulls, hurled themselves again and again at the same point in the enemy lines. They did make some impression, too, though at fantastic cost. With rifle and bayonet, bombs, knuckledusters, and knives the three Canadian

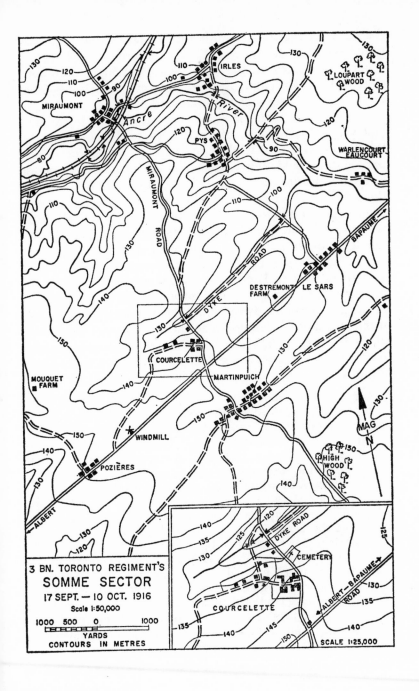

3 BN. TORONTO REGIMENT'S
SOMME SECTOR
17 SEPT. — 10 OCT. 1916
Scale 1:50,000

1000 500 0 1000
YARDS
CONTOURS IN METRES

divisions fought for a month for the possession of a few trenches hardly distinguishable on the ground and seldom accurately located on the map. Some Canadian battalions were down to a strength of seventy-five men, and the number of shellshock cases steadily increased.

The nerves of some men broke completely, and it was staff policy at G.H.Q. to make examples of cases of alleged cowardice. Every once in a while a battalion in rest billets would parade in the cold grey dawn to witness the execution of one of its men before a firing squad. When the squad had fired, the officer in charge had to make sure that the prisoner was dead; if not, it was the officer's duty to shoot him in the head with his revolver. In at least one case the officer refused and told the provost marshal in attendance "to do his own bloody work". He was at once arrested.

If there were isolated cases of cowardice, there were infinitely more instances of gallantry and self-sacrifice, many of them never officially recognized. One case that was recognized was that of eighteen-year-old Piper James Richardson of the 16th (Canadian Scottish) Battalion, who was awarded the Victoria Cross for his conduct at Regina Trench on the 8th of October. The official citation read:

> For most conspicuous bravery and devotion to duty when, prior to attack, he obtained permission from his Commanding Officer to play his company "over the top". As the company approached the objective, it was held up by very strong wire and came under intense fire, which caused heavy casualties and demoralized the formation for the moment. Realizing the situation, Piper Richardson strode up and down outside the wire playing his pipes with the greatest coolness. The effect was instantaneous. Inspired by his splendid example, the company rushed the wire with such fury and determination that the obstacle was overcome and the position captured. Later, after participating in bombing operations, he was detailed to take back a wounded comrade and prisoners. After proceeding about 200 yards Piper Richardson remembered that he had left his pipes behind. Although strongly urged not to do so, he insisted on returning to recover his pipes. He has never been seen since, and death has been presumed accordingly owing to lapse of time.

Lord Cavan, the commander of the XIV British Corps, was

one of the few senior officers to protest against the futility of further attacks. Perhaps even in wartime there were advantages to being an earl. At all events, he not only protested but added a sharply pointed comment: "No one who has not visited the front can really know the state of exhaustion to which the men are reduced."

The enemy suffered too. Perhaps by now he suffered equally. At lunchtime, in their châteaux behind the lines, senior commanders and their staff officers assured anxious politicians and newspaper correspondents that the enemy's casualties far exceeded our own. They had always said this; some of them, after the war, wrote books to prove it, although their information then was no better than it had been during the battle. The British, French, and German casualty statistics for the Somme were never accurately computed, and no one knows to this day exactly how many men died, were wounded, or disappeared. What can be said is that on both sides some three million soldiers fought in the battle and that over a million were casualties of one sort or another.

On October 11 the 3rd Canadian Division was relieved in the line by Major-General D. Watson's 4th Canadian Division, and six days later the 1st, 2nd, and 3rd divisions left the Somme for the Vimy Ridge area. The 4th Division and the Canadian artillery remained until the end of November, during which time they captured Regina and Desire trenches. In November, after a final series of abortive attacks in freezing temperatures and driving snow, Haig called off the battle. When the Canadian infantry at last came out of the line and marched the four miles to the nearest bivouacs at Tara Hill, they were so coated with half-frozen mud that a man's clothing, boots, and puttees sometimes weighed 120 pounds.

Towards the end of the year in another conference at Chantilly, Joffre and Haig agreed that the Somme offensive should be renewed in the spring. Before then, however, Joffre was relieved of his command and Ludendorff frustrated Haig's plans by evacuating the whole Somme area and falling back to the newly constructed Hindenburg Line. This move shortened the German front by thirty-two miles and released fourteen German divisions for employment elsewhere.

Even today the results of the Somme are a matter of some

controversy. Haig's apologists claim that, by relieving Verdun, the battle saved France and, by wearing down the German army, virtually won the war. Others point to the admittedly inaccurate official casualty figures – British, 419,654; French, 204,253; German, 465,525 – and argue that this was an excessive price to pay for a maximum Allied gain of eight miles along a twelve-mile front.*

The second school of thought would seem to have the better reasons on its side. Certainly no soldier would claim that a major war between great powers can be fought without much bloodshed. The German army could not be defeated without hard fighting. But for the intelligent soldier hard fighting is a means to an end, not an end in itself. He attempts always to fight when the odds are in his favour, when surprise, or the nature of the ground, or a superiority of numbers or weapons, or some other factor gives him the probability of success. The whole art of war is so to stage-manage the battle that, when it occurs, victory is the reward. The trouble with attempting to wear out your enemy in a brutal slogging match is that you wear yourself out at least equally. The commanding general of a great national army has entrusted to his care the nation's most valuable asset, the lives of his men. It is his high and tragic duty to spend some of those lives to purchase victory. When he squanders them stupidly, wastefully, and heedlessly he is betraying his trust. At the Somme there was never any hope of winning victory. The choice of the battlefield and the selection of the aim of the battle determined this from the outset. The preparations were conducted with a complete disregard of the possibility of surprise. The plan was utterly inflexible. The Allied resources, great as they were, were inadequate for the chosen task and, as in the case of the artillery support, were not sufficiently concentrated.

These criticisms are all of a general nature and are sufficiently serious to explain the deplorable result. When we look more closely at the actual conduct of the operation, we see that the stupidity of the tactics employed would certainly

* The German casualty figures did not include the slightly wounded who could soon return to duty.

have ruined even a plan that was strategically brilliant. The first day's disaster determined the course of the battle. It should, in fact, have ended the battle. Thereafter it was always much easier for the Germans to reinforce by rail than for the British to advance across country. After July 1 it was merely a matter of measuring out blood for blood. If further attacks were really necessary "to save the French", they should have been launched elsewhere and differently. But what could be expected of a commander and staff that had perpetrated the 1st of July? The lack of imagination, the inability to come to grips with reality, the stubborn clinging to delusion in the face of repeated, bitter experience – these qualities had been manifested long before and Haig had obviously learned nothing since he had lectured the commander and staff of the 1st Canadian Division in the little headquarters room at Festubert.

Between September and November at the Somme the 77,000 Canadians had advanced 3,000 yards for a loss of 24,029 men, about one-third of whom were killed. Officers and men had fought magnificently, had performed countless acts of heroism, and had undergone an ordeal not to be surpassed until they were committed to the mud of Passchendaele in the autumn of 1917.

The year 1916 had been the most bloodstained in history. On the Western Front the Allies had failed at the Somme and the Germans at Verdun. In Italy the Eighth Battle of the Isonzo had ended like the preceding seven – in stalemate. In the east the Russians had suffered gigantic losses and Romania had fallen. The Allies had achieved some minor success in the Cameroons and in German East Africa. As the year drew to a close, the effects of the British naval blockade were being increasingly felt in Germany and the Kaiser was under heavy pressure to sanction unrestricted U-boat warfare, even at the risk of bringing the United States into the conflict. Neither side any longer fought for victory, or at least not in the sense they had fought for victory in 1914. The essence of victory is that something is won. By the end of 1916 all the belligerents had lost so much that no conceivable gains could be adequate compensation. Both sides now fought for survival.

It would have been a reasonable time to make peace. The Pope was of that opinion, and so were Lord Lansdowne, a former governor general of Canada, President Wilson of the United States, and German Chancellor Bethmann-Holweg. In 1917 each of these men tried, in his own way, to bring about a negotiated peace, but there was no hope that their counsels of moderation would be heeded. Too much blood had been shed and too much hatred unleashed. The belligerents used the winter as a breathing spell, preparing for the spring when they could continue with the destruction of Europe.

After the Somme the Canadians moved north to Artois where they took over a quiet sector of the line between Arras and Lens. Here they improved their defences, trained, and conducted trench raids to keep the offensive spirit alive. The Allied high command, after long reflection, had evolved a plan for 1917 – it would continue the Battle of the Somme on a wider front. However, the French nation, which had suffered more severely than the British, had less patience with its generals. Joffre was relieved of his command in December 1916 and General Robert Nivelle, who had made a name for himself at Verdun, became general-in-chief. Nivelle announced his intention of winning the war in the spring with a single massive blow along the Aisne. When the Germans suddenly withdrew to the Hindenburg Line in March, thereby shortening their line and freeing fourteen divisions for employment elsewhere, Nivelle made only minor adjustments to his plan.

As a preliminary to the Nivelle offensive, Field Marshal Haig* was to attack about Arras to draw off German reserves and outflank the Hindenburg Line. The British offensive was to be on a twelve-mile front, employing three corps of General Sir E. Allenby's Third Army, while on the extreme left, the Canadian Corps of General Sir H. S. Horne's First Army was to capture the Vimy Ridge.

The ridge ran from the northwest to the southeast between Lens and Arras. The main height of land was four miles long, with its highest point only 475 feet above sea level, but its command of the valley of the Scarpe River and the Douai Plain made it an important tactical feature. The Germans had held it since 1914, and three French attacks in 1914 and 1915 had failed to dislodge them. Already more than 200,000 men had fallen on the long, gentle slopes leading up to the crest.

The Germans were therefore understandably confident that, whatever other portion of the line might be in danger,

* King George V, on his own initiative, had promoted Haig to field marshal at the beginning of 1917. The British cabinet had not been consulted, for the King regarded the promotion "as a New Year's gift from myself and the country".

Vimy Ridge could certainly be held. The elderly commander of the German Sixth Army, General von Falkenhausen, whose responsibility it was, felt supremely confident. He had three strong defensive lines, just as von Below had had on the Somme, and his one Prussian and two Bavarian divisions on the ridge were every bit as good as von Below's troops had been.

Von Falkenhausen was not a man who readily accepted new ideas. Other German soldiers – notably a certain Colonel Fritz von Lossberg, who was proving himself something of a defensive genius – had studied the Battle of the Somme with a critical eye and learned much from it. Lossberg's new tactical doctrine had been made available to General Falkenhausen in pamphlets, but it is doubtful whether he read them. Certainly he chose to ignore the new-fangled ideas they advocated, such as flexibility in the defence, the positioning of reserves close behind the second line for counterattack, and the deepening of the battle zone so that the main line of resistance would be out of range of the attacker's field artillery. Von Falkenhausen put his faith in rigid trench lines well covered by wire, in good, deep dugouts, and in machine guns and artillery. He kept only five regiments actually on the ridge, and in many of these the rifle companies were at half strength. Support battalions were in the third line and the reserve battalions were two hours' march from the front. His five reserve divisions were ten to twenty-five miles away, well out of reach of shellfire. Such dispositions had been more than adequate in 1916.

But the Canadians, too, had learned from their bitter experience at the Somme. During the quiet winter in Artois General Currie had drawn some definite conclusions about attacks on fortified lines, and he disseminated these to senior Canadian commanders and staff officers in a series of valuable lectures. As a result, the attack on Vimy Ridge was to be very different from those on the Somme the previous autumn. The differences, it is true, were mainly technical, the modification and improvement of existing tactics, rather than any startling new concept, but they were to prove sufficient.

For weeks before the battle the Royal Flying Corps continually photographed the German positions; a new sound-ranging technique was introduced to locate enemy batteries; and, above all, the Canadian infantry fought for information in a series of trench raids which began on March 20 and continued nightly until the attack. These raids were expensive – the Canadians lost 1,400 men in two weeks – but they did keep headquarters in touch with reality. Every night Canadian soldiers with blackened faces crawled out into no-man's-land, wormed their way face-up through the enemy wire, silently killed German sentries, saw what they had been sent to see, and returned to report. Sometimes they brought back prisoners for interrogation, and very often they had to carry in their own wounded.

Although the plan for the capture of Vimy Ridge was worked out to the last detail, it was not drafted entirely from maps as though it were a theoretical staff exercise. Senior officers spent long hours studying the ground, and battalion commanders, company commanders, and even subalterns were encouraged to comment on their part in the operation and to make suggestions for improvements. Never before in the war had an Allied attack been planned with such care and such common sense. The point about common sense is important, for up until now it had been a virtue little in evidence in this war. At the Second Battle of Ypres, at Festubert, at Givenchy, and at the Somme, if a fact had clashed with a theory, more often than not it had been the fact that was discarded.

At army headquarters at Lillers unit officers studied a large-scale plasticine model of the ridge which showed with amazing accuracy each small contour and fold in the ground. Behind the line, on the rolling downland west of the high road known as the Chaussée Brunehaut, between Estrée Cauchie and Les Quatre Vents, a full-scale replica of the German defences on Vimy Ridge was laid out on the ground, marked with white tapes and coloured flags. Trenches, roads, machine-gun emplacements, and strong-points were accurately located from air photographs. Vimy village, Farbus Wood, von Loën Weg, Island Traverse, Zwischen Stellung, Nine Elms, Commandant's House, Thélus village, La Folie Farm, the Orchard, and the Pimple were all drawn out to scale. Day after day the attacking battalions practised on this replica until each man knew, not only his own task, but also the tasks of those in his immediate vicinity.

And every day, mixing freely with the troops, the quiet friendly figure of General Byng could be seen, going over the area with the battalions, explaining details, encouraging, watching, assessing. The Canadians took to Byng. They liked his casual way of returning salutes, his unpretentious manner, and his obvious common sense. When they saw him squatting on the ground, drawing diagrams in the dirt for the officers clustered around him, the soldiers felt a new confidence.

The artillery under Brigadier-General E. W. B. Morrison had 377 heavy and 720 field guns for the preliminary bombardment, about twice the number that had been available at the Somme for the same frontage of attack. For seven days before the assault a continuous rain of high explosive pounded the German defences. The shells streamed over the Canadian trenches "like water from a hose", but the fire was selective, not merely a mass saturation. Strong-points were destroyed, villages levelled, and communication trenches raked with shrapnel. The Germans later referred to this period as "the week of suffering". Some units did not receive rations, ammunition, or reliefs for three or four days, so that by April 9, when the attack was launched, their men were almost starving. A new fuse, the 106, which had been especially developed to cut wire, worked well, and the enemy was given no chance to repair his demolished entanglements. Counter-battery techniques were brought to a new perfection; of the 212 German guns on the Canadian front, 83 per cent were located and destroyed before zero hour.

Everyone was so busy preparing for the attack that scant attention was paid to world events. However, these were not without interest. On February 27 revolution broke out in Petrograd, the Russian capital, and on March 2 the Tsar abdicated. An almost immediate effect of the Russian revolution was to relieve the pressure on Germany's Eastern Front. Russia remained formally in the war for the time being and no large-scale German troop withdrawals were yet possible, but the war in the east ceased to be a matter of pressing anxiety to the German supreme command. On April 6 the

United States declared war on Germany. Eventually this would more than offset the loss of Russia to the Allied cause, but it would be at least a year before any sizable number of American troops would be ready to fight in Europe.

Meanwhile, in the skies above Vimy Ridge, the Royal Flying Corps, although equipped with planes inferior to the new German Albatrosses, worked heroically before the battle, directing the artillery, taking photographs, and registering targets. Many Allied fliers were shot down in dogfights, several of them by a brilliant scarlet Albatross flown by Baron von Richthofen.

The Canadian attack was planned in four phases, with successive objectives being given the code names of the Black, Red, Blue, and Brown lines. The four divisions were aligned in numerical order from right to left, each attacking with two brigades in the first line and one in support. The British 5th Division was placed under General Byng as a corps reserve, but its 13th Brigade had an active role in the final phase. Since Vimy Ridge ran aslant the axis of attack, the corps's right wing had farther to go than its left, 4,000 yards as opposed to 700, and only the 1st and 2nd divisions would take part in the last two phases.

Through the chill night of April 8–9 a Canadian infantry battalion marched along the road that led from the ruins of Neuville St. Vaast. The dark, anonymous figures in the long column were silhouetted against a landscape silvered by a low moon nearly at the full. Suddenly, under the bright sky, the leading platoon disappeared. One moment it was there, swinging along the road at the foot of a little hill. The next instant it seemed to march directly into the hillside, as the children did who followed the Pied Piper. Two minutes later the second platoon had also vanished.

It was not an optical illusion. The road ended abruptly at the hillside and became a tunnel sloping steeply down into the earth. Near the entrance of this underground passage a dim electric light bulb revealed revetted chalk walls and a beaten chalk floor. The tunnel led downward for about fifty yards, then levelled off at a depth of forty feet to run almost due east for half a mile. Since the soldiers could not march along this narrow subterranean route in fours, they broke step and, crowding slightly together, went on by twos and threes, their rifles slung from their shoulders. Every twenty yards or so, when they passed a light bulb, they cast huge, distorted shadows on the dead white walls. The smell of chalk was sharp in their nostrils, stirring incongruous memories of schoolrooms and blackboards.

The Zivy Tunnel, along which the soldiers were proceeding, ran from reserve positions in the 2nd Canadian Division's sector to the front line at the foot of Vimy Ridge. It was equipped with electricity, water mains, and a small tramway. Branching galleries and rooms off the main passageway contained the 4th Brigade headquarters, signal offices, ammunition dumps, an advanced dressing station with emergency operating tables and chicken-wire bunks, and a battalion headquarters. An ancient underground quarry, which formed a great cave near the end of the tunnel, was large enough to shelter a whole battalion.

That night, across the four-mile front of the Canadian Corps, men marched into eleven similar tunnels that led to

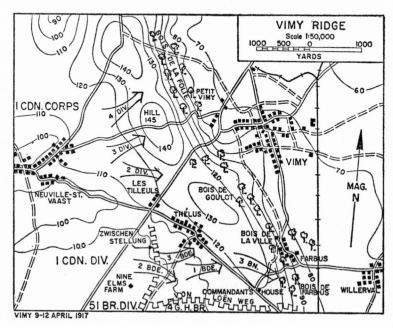

VIMY 9-12 APRIL 1917

the line. Then they waited, temporarily safe in the tunnels and caves near the battle zone, each man busy with his own thoughts. There was no room to lie down, so the soldiers sat hunched on the floor, awkward in their greatcoats, webbing, tin hats, and battle equipment. The caves were permeated with the unmistakable odour of the army, a composite smell dominated by the reek of damp khaki-wool uniforms. Some men played poker by the flickering light of candles, pledging high stakes on slips of paper that might never be redeemed; some tried to sleep; some sought out unit chaplains to make their whispered confessions. In the course of the night a hot meal was served and everyone received a welcome ration of rum.

Other Canadians had less adequate accommodation. Many units filed quietly into forward trenches, guided through the darkness by posts that gleamed on one side with luminous paint. Some companies crept out into no-man's-land to shell holes and ditches within a hundred yards of the nearest German outposts. By the appointed time every infantry battalion in the Canadian Corps was in position, with each man waiting, silent and tense, for zero hour. After midnight the sky clouded over and a cold wind with sleet in it began to blow from the northwest.

By four o'clock on the morning of Easter Monday, the 9th, all forty-eight Canadian battalions, some 30,000 men, were in position, ready to go over the top. Enemy headquarters had no idea that the attack would soon be launched; von Falkenhausen did not expect it for another week. By now a sharp frost had set in, hardening the mud and covering the puddles with ice that starred and crackled underfoot like breaking glass. The clouded sky held in the darkness after dawn, but the Canadians had rehearsed so well that this was no drawback.

Bayonets were fixed with a series of clicks that echoed along the crowded trenches. Officers stared at the luminous dials of their wristwatches. Then, sharp at 5.30, every gun in the Canadian sector spoke at once and two mines were blown under the left portion of the German front. Vimy Ridge seemed to erupt into the air as gouts of earth, sandbags, and bits of wood were tossed upwards by the shellfire.

Ten seconds later hundreds of red, white, and green rockets soared up from the German lines and fountains of golden fire played above the ridge as the enemy frantically called for support from his artillery. However, because of the effective Canadian counter-battery fire the German guns made only a weak response. The attacking battalions rose and walked into the blackness, leaning hard against their barrage which moved forward at 100-yard intervals.

On the right, where the 2nd and 3rd brigades of Currie's 1st Division advanced with three battalions each, the Canadians were at the German first line before the dazed enemy soldiers clambered out of their dugouts. The sentries who had remained above ground were quickly bayoneted, and squads of bombers were left at the dugout entrances to stand guard until the next wave of Canadians arrived to mop up. The attackers pushed on.

At the second trench there was some sharp hand-to-hand fighting, although most of the resistance here came from snipers and brave machine-gun crews. By 6.15, only forty-five minutes after zero hour, the 1st and 2nd divisions reported themselves securely on the Black Line, and battalion headquarters began moving out to occupy forward positions in shell holes and captured enemy dugouts. Ten minutes later the 7th and 8th brigades of Major-General Lipsett's 3rd Division also reported the first phase successfully completed. Only on the extreme left, where Major-General Watson's 4th Division was to capture Hill 145 and a feature known as the Pimple, did the attack run into serious difficulties. Here heavy machine-gun fire cut down many Canadians and the attackers were often taken from the rear by Germans who unexpectedly popped up behind them out of mine shafts and assembly trenches. The fighting on the 4th Division's front continued to be confused and bitter throughout the day.

Elsewhere the Canadians swept victoriously on, exactly according to timetable. The reserve companies of the 1st Division's battalions passed through the Black Line at 6.45 and were in among the Bavarians manning the German second position before they knew it. The enemy, half blinded by driving snow and smoke drifting down from the burning village of Thélus, retreated towards Farbus Wood in disorder.

In the captured German dugouts the Canadians found large stocks of soda water and hundreds of loaves of black bread too heavy and sour to be eaten. The left half of the division's objective on the Red Line was captured by seven o'clock, and after a brief fight the right portion was also taken.

The 2nd Division did equally well. The 21st (Eastern Ontario) Battalion routed out 106 bewildered Germans from a large cave beneath the ruins of Les Tilleuls, and the 25th Battalion (Nova Scotia Rifles) captured the trench known as Turko-Graben. So far, casualties had been extremely light, being far exceeded by the number of prisoners taken.

By 7.30 the 3rd Division reached the crest of Vimy Ridge and reported its final objectives gained. As the troops moved into the western portion of the Bois de la Folie on the reverse slope they saw hundreds of Germans in full retreat downhill. Machine-gun fire cut some of them down and hastened the remainder on their way. When it was learned at nine o'clock that Hill 145 had not been captured, the 7th Brigade established a defensive flank from the Bois de la Folie to the original front line.

At ten o'clock the barrage lifted again and the 1st and 2nd divisions moved on to the Blue Line which ran along the crest of the Ridge. The ruins of Thélus village looked directly down on the advancing soldiers, but no fire came from that direction. The long lines of khaki-clad figures walked slowly uphill, well spread out in artillery formation but keeping constant pace with the shell-bursts ahead of them.

Near Thélus village some men of the 31st (Alberta) Battalion discovered an entrance to a dugout and went down to investigate. They descended the earthen steps cautiously, Mills bombs in their hands, ready for opposition. At the foot of the steps they pushed back the canvas curtain and found a spacious room set up as an officers' mess. Candle-lit tables gleamed with linen and silver, a well-stocked bar stood in one corner, and five white-coated mess waiters, their hands above their heads, cowered against the wall. The Canadians took time for a quick drink, then went on their way.

Suddenly – almost unexpectedly – the soldiers reached the top of the ridge. A fresh wind swept the crest, blowing away the smoke of the barrage and dispelling the wisps of morning mist that had limited their vision during the climb. At that moment the sun broke through the clouds, bathing the scene in bright, golden light. The Canadians found themselves looking down over an unbelievable panorama of enemy-occupied territory. No Germans were in the immediate locality, but far down the wooden reverse slopes little groups of grey figures were hurrying eastward in full retreat. The two sides of the ridge provided a striking contrast, and one that was perhaps symbolic. The attackers had crossed a muddy waste of desolation to reach the crest, but now below them a fertile countryside stretched out mile after mile, with red-roofed houses and trees just turning green, all untouched by the ravages of war.

For an hour and a half the Canadians halted on the top of Vimy Ridge, digging in, setting up machine guns, evacuating their wounded, bringing up supplies, and reorganizing. Then the barrage, which had stood still all this while in front of them, lifted for the last time, and fresh troops passed through to take the final objective of the day. In Farbus Wood where a battery of enemy guns was overrun, Canadian soldiers, who had been especially trained for just this eventuality, turned the gun muzzles to the east and opened fire.

Farther north the 6th Brigade found enemy machine guns and artillery pieces still firing in the Bois de la Ville. The 27th (City of Winnipeg) Battalion and the 29th (Vancouver) Battalion sent a shower of rifle grenades in among the defenders, then charged wildly downhill to clear the wood with the bayonet. Two hundred and fifty prisoners were taken, including the commander of the 3rd Bavarian Reserve Regiment and his staff. The Winnipeg men had somehow managed to bring pots of green paint with them and with this they painted their unit designation, a rectangle with a circle above it, on the backs of prisoners, so that no one could argue about which unit should be credited with the capture.

Late in the afternoon, under cold skies already touched with the grey of an early evening, two cavalry patrols of the Canadian Light Horse cantered out of Farbus village towards Willerval, a mile to the east. Their task was to discover the extent of the German withdrawal. Since this was 1917, they looked very different from the glittering troopers of other days. They wore the same round tin hats as the infantry and carried rifles rather than lances; only their breeches, spurs, and leather bandoliers showed that they belonged to a mounted arm. Unfortunately, a man on horseback presented all too large a target, and before the Canadian Light Horse reached Willerval one patrol lost half its men and horses to a machine gun sited on a farmhouse roof and the other patrol was practically annihilated by rifle fire.

Only on the extreme left, where the enemy was valiantly defending Hill 145 and the Pimple, were the day's objectives not completely taken. Here, after repeated attacks, three Canadian battalions cleared the western side of Hill 145, although they suffered heavy losses in doing so. Farther north the 12th Brigade captured the first German trench easily, but only bitter fighting drove the Germans from their second line. On April 12, however, four battalions went irresistibly forward with a raging snowstorm at their backs and swept the Germans from their last positions. On the hard-won Pimple Canadian machine-gunners hastily set up their guns and opened fire on the fleeing enemy, and in a brief spell of sunshine they could see German guns and limbers being galloped madly away along the Lens-Arras road. An elderly French interpreter, who accompanied the Canadians, stood on the hilltop, tears running down his face into his iron-grey beard as he looked out across the plain towards his native Douai which he had not seen since 1914.

That same day Crown Prince Rupprecht of Bavaria, the German army group commander, ordered a withdrawal to a new line two miles and more to the rear of Vimy Ridge. Shortly afterwards General von Falkenhausen was removed from active command and appointed military governor of Belgium. General Byng, on the other hand, was promoted to command an army, and General Currie succeeded him as commander of the Canadian Corps.

Undoubtedly the capture of Vimy Ridge had been the greatest British victory of the war up to that time. The Canadians had advanced two and a half miles, had captured 54 guns, 104 trench mortars, 124 machine guns, and more than 4,000 prisoners. The British Third Army, attacking to the south, had done almost as well, although not all its final objectives were taken. General Ludendorff, who had celebrated his fifty-second birthday on April 9, confessed that he was "deeply depressed" by the loss of Vimy Ridge.

The Canadian Corps had demonstrated not only that successful attacks were possible but also that with proper planning they did not have to be prohibitively expensive. In the fighting at Vimy, total Canadian casualties were 10,602, of which 3,598 were fatal. These casualties were by no means light, but they were far lighter than those of any previous offensive.

It is certainly not meant to detract from the splendour of the Canadian achievement to suggest that the importance of the battle was somewhat exaggerated. The Allies badly needed a victory for psychological reasons and for this purpose the capture of Vimy Ridge seemed in every way made to order. The ridge itself was an imposing natural feature, something men could plainly see and which their understanding could encompass without the aid of a map. Moreover, it had been captured by the Canadians, not by a major ally, and so praise did not need to be filtered through jealousy. In any case, the Allied world was generous in its acclaim. The French press spoke of the capture of the ridge as an Easter gift from Canada to the French nation; King George V said that "Canada will be proud that the taking of the coveted Vimy Ridge has fallen to the lot of her troops"; and the First Army commander attributed the Canadian success to "soundness of plan, thoroughness of preparation, dash and determination in execution, and devotion to duty on the part of all concerned".

All this was most undoubtedly true. Nevertheless, certain other things must be mentioned as well. In the first place, the enemy's mistakes contributed substantially to the Canadian success. The tactics of the German Sixth Army at Vimy were the tactics of the Somme, and against these the Canadians had devised an adequate answer. It is interesting to note that what most deeply disturbed Ludendorff about the fall of Vimy Ridge was the fear that the new German defensive tactics had been tried and found wanting. He was immensely reassured when post-battle analysis revealed that von Falkenhausen had, in fact, found the new tactics difficult to comprehend and had left them untried. The Canadian plan of attack was wonderfully careful and detailed but it was also somewhat inflexible. It was basically a gunner's plan. Everything depended on the artillery, for it was really the guns that captured the ground and the infantry who occupied it. This worked well in April 1917 against an enemy who was still using the defensive methods of 1916, but it was not an infallible key to success in battle. A fair assessment of the capture of Vimy Ridge would be that the plan had been sound but not brilliant. But by April 1917 a sound plan looked, by mere contrast, to be the product of military genius.

The Canadian Corps was to win other outstanding victories in the war, some of them inherently more important, but none so caught the popular imagination or were so peculiarly identified with Canada as the taking of Vimy Ridge. As is usually the case in such matters, this popular instinct was absolutely right. No matter what the constitutional historians may say, it was on Easter Monday, April 9, 1917, and not on any other date, that Canada became a nation.

In the Memorial Chamber of the Peace Tower in Ottawa there is a simple marble plaque that reads:

> THEY ARE TOO NEAR
> TO BE GREAT
> BUT OUR CHILDREN
> SHALL UNDERSTAND
> WHERE AND HOW OUR
> FATE WAS CHANGED
> AND BY WHOSE HAND

And it is fitting that Canada's greatest memorial to her fallen sons should stand on ground ceded in perpetuity by France to Canada, on the top of Hill 145, the highest point of Vimy Ridge.

General Robert Nivelle was an eloquent man and full of confidence. His eloquence enabled him to overcome the doubts of the French government about his offensive and his confidence enabled him to brush aside as unimportant the fact that Ludendorff had learned the details of his attack from captured French orders. The Nivelle offensive began on April 16, and it was a murderous failure. French casualties in the first ten days of the battle numbered 134,000.

On April 23 Haig launched a diversionary attack astride the Scarpe to help the French. A brief period of heavy fighting followed and only slight gains were made, but Haig attacked again on April 28 with five divisions on a six-mile front. One of the assaulting formations was the 1st Canadian Division which was given the task of attacking the Arleux Loop, an enemy salient in front of the village of Arleux-en-Gohelle. Like the French offensive, this new British attack was everywhere a disastrous fiasco, except in the Canadian sector where the 2nd Brigade took Arleux and achieved what the British official historian described as "the only tangible success of the whole operation".

By now the French armies on the Aisne were deeply committed and Haig launched another diversionary attack on May 3 in an attempt to help them. The battleground chosen was again the Scarpe and again the results were the same. The British suffered grievous losses and failed everywhere, except for the Canadian Corps's sector where the 1st and 6th brigades captured the village of Fresnoy. This, said the British official historian, was "the relieving feature of a day which many who witnessed it considered the blackest of the War". Unfortunately, after the Canadians handed Fresnoy over to the British, it was recaptured by a German counterattack on May 8.

In the meanwhile, Nivelle's offensive was petering out. The French had made a maximum gain of about four miles but their attacks north and east of Reims had won virtually no ground at all. And French casualties had been about 200,000.

For nearly three years the French army had been heavily engaged; all through 1914 and 1915 it had borne the brunt of the fighting on the Western Front; and almost an entire generation of French youth had perished. With the collapse of the Nivelle offensive, French morale cracked. Battalions refused to go to the front; units deserted en masse; staff officers, who were called *les buveurs du sang*, were attacked; mutineers, singing "The Internationale", seized railway trains and stations; and by the end of May there was mutiny in fifty-four French divisions. Soldiers' councils were formed in French battalions, officers could exercise no authority, and by June there were, between the French front and Paris, only two French divisions that could be relied upon. The situation in Paris was even worse. Deserting soldiers and those on leave were met at the railway stations and given pacifist propaganda; strikes and riots broke out; the left-wing political parties agitated for an end to the war; at least one Paris newspaper, which preached a doctrine of surrender, was owned by the German government through a Swiss holding company; defeatism and, worse than defeatism, outright treason infected some members of the Chamber of Deputies. It all looked very much like what had happened in Russia in the spring, and many of the French agitators undoubtedly hoped for a similar outcome.

The French government replaced Nivelle with General Henri Philippe Pétain, known as the Saviour of Verdun, but in the early summer of 1917 France was, to all intents and purposes, temporarily out of the war. Haig was fully informed of this situation but, with a very peculiar conception of his responsibilities as British commander-in-chief, he chose to regard the French mutinies as a military secret which he was not at liberty to divulge to his own government. He decided to launch a great offensive in Belgium, break out of the Ypres Salient, capture the German submarine bases at Ostend and Zeebrugge, roll up the German right flank, and win the war single-handed. He wrote to Field Marshal Sir William Robertson, the Chief of the Imperial General Staff: "For the last two years most of us soldiers have realized that Great Britain must take the necessary steps to win the war by herself, because our French allies had already shown that they lacked both the moral qualities and the means of gaining victory." In order to divert the enemy's attention from Flanders and prevent him from moving his reserves, he ordered the Canadian Corps to attack in Artois.

On July 7, General Currie was instructed to make a straightforward frontal assault against the town of Lens itself. However, Currie had always believed in looking at the ground before undertaking an operation. He climbed the Bois de l'Hirondelle spur, lay down in the tall grass, and spent an entire morning studying the proposed battlefield with minute care. What he saw was not encouraging. To his front sprawled the ugly industrial town of Lens, deserted by its inhabitants now although it had had a population of 30,000 before the war. To the north and east stretched the wreckage of one of France's most important mining districts — huge slag heaps like truncated cones, pitheads, collieries, the black towers of fosses, and tangled railway sidings. North of Lens the Cité spur was covered with the ruins of little red-brick company towns clustered like poor relations on both sides of the Arras–La Bassée road. Even in peacetime, Cité St. Laurent, Cité St. Emile, and Cité Ste. Elisabeth had been eyesores; now they were mere heaps of rubble and charred rafters, mazed with trenches, barbed wire, and machine-gun posts. What was even worse was that Lens was overlooked from the north by Hill 70, about a mile and a half away from the centre of the town, and from the southeast by Sallaumines Hill. Although Hill 70 was only a bare chalk down, rising gently and almost imperceptibly above the Artois countryside, it gave a commanding view of Lens and the Douai Plain. Its northern slope was broken by two woods, the Bois Rasé and the Bois Hugo, and by a large chalk quarry. Currie had no difficulty in deciding that it was Hill 70, not the ruins of Lens, that was the vital ground in the area.

A frontal assault on Lens itself would take the Canadians into nasty, close country and, even if the attack were successful, the troops would merely have been thrust into a trap where they would be mercilessly shelled by encircling German guns. Moreover, to support the attack the Canadian artillery would have to move farther out into the plain. Currie went at once to First Army headquarters, confronted General Horne, the army commander, and told him that Hill 70 would be a more rational objective. This by itself was unusual behaviour for a newly promoted corps commander, but Currie was blunt about it. He even added: "If we have to fight at all, let us fight for something worth having."

Before the matter was settled, the British commander-in-chief was brought into the discussion, and Haig finally agreed to amend the plan as Currie wished, although he warned the Canadian that "the Boche would not let us have Hill 70". Currie agreed that the Germans would make strenuous efforts to retain or retake the hill, but he was confident that the well-sited Canadian artillery would be able to break up the enemy counterattacks.

Before the battle began there was to be yet one more example of the mindless interference of higher headquarters in the tactical details of operations, and Currie had one more disagreement with his superiors. When ordered to make a diversionary attack south of Lens, he planned, not a full-scale assault, but only a one-battalion raid with the attacking troops withdrawing at the completion of the operation. First Army headquarters at once reminded him of Haig's recent grandiloquent order that captured ground "must be held, by rifle and bayonet alone if no assistance is obtained from other arms". Currie, however, was not intimidated; he pointed out the obvious fact that the area in question was commanded from in front and enfiladed from both flanks; and his final orders remained unchanged – to raid and withdraw. As a result, the attack, which was carried out by the

116th Battalion on July 23, was a complete tactical success, although it did not fulfil its intended function of deceiving the enemy.

The assault on Hill 70 was planned as carefully as the capture of Vimy Ridge had been. Taped replicas of the battlefield were set up at Aix Noulette, Marqueffles Farm, and Marzingarbe, and the troops rehearsed until they were thoroughly familiar with their tasks. The area around Hill 70 had seen some of the bloodiest fighting of the war. The Canadians marched in along the Lens-Béthune road, through Le Philosophe, past Quality Street, through the old front line of 1915 and the ruins of Loos, where so many thousands had died. Two years previously, the British had taken Hill 70, had held it briefly, and had been driven off again. Now the Germans, who were expecting the Canadian attack, hoped for a similar outcome. Bad weather and the necessity of regrouping the artillery postponed the opening of the battle and, of course, the enemy discovered what was afoot. Even the date of the assault was known beforehand to the German high command.

At 4.25 in the morning of August 15, 1917, one or two pale stars still shone in the sky above Arras when the Canadian barrage suddenly roared out and the leading companies hoisted themselves over the parapet of the jumping-off trench. In the sector allotted to one of the Canadian Scottish battalions a few isolated figures strutted in front of the foremost riflemen, and through the noise of the guns there sounded from time to time the high, shrilling skirl of a Highland air. The pipers strode proudly on, their kilts swinging and their bagpipes tucked under their arms, as unconcerned as though they were playing at a clan reunion in some quiet Ontario glen. Behind them the riflemen stepped out smartly, for it would never do to let the makers of that wild music reach the enemy lines alone.

It was light enough to see perhaps fifty yards, but the eastern horizon was already streaked with scarlet and before long a machine-gunner would be able to take aim from a quarter of a mile. The way led gently uphill through a shattered wood, the Bois Rasé, towards the crest of Hill 70, just north of Lens. The previous night the enemy, nervous about the assault he knew was coming, had sent over a number of gas shells, but now the German guns were slow to answer the frantic calls from their front-line infantry. It was three minutes before the German artillery began firing its defensive tasks, and by then the Canadian assault had passed on.

As far as a man could see, Canadian soldiers were walking forward over the shell-torn ground. The 1st and 2nd divisions were each assaulting with two brigades, a total of ten attacking battalions, or some 7,000 men. The lines of advancing infantrymen extended for two miles, south from the Bois Hugo to the outskirts of Lens.

The Canadian guns were shooting beautifully, the black shell-bursts falling as straight as a ruler along the German front. Behind the barrage, which was being fired by 204 eighteen-pounders, the enemy support positions were being pounded by medium and heavy guns, and away on the right the Royal Engineers were projecting great drums of burning oil into Cité Ste. Elisabeth. The oil drums hurtled through the air with a peculiar whirring sound and burst in pools of hissing flame and clouds of oily black smoke.

As the Canadians approached the broken German wire, they could see their shells falling into the front trench, making it look like a trough filled with shaking light. They found the first position blown to pieces; dead bodies lay buried under fallen parapets, wounded Germans screamed in the bottom of the trench, and a few grey-clad figures could be seen scurrying back to the rear. The enemy who remained showed little fight, and with scarcely a pause the Canadians pushed on to their first objective, the Blue Line. On the left Major-General A. C. Macdonell's 1st Division occupied the crest of Hill 70 and the open country east of the Arras–La Bassée road. On the right Major-General Burstall's 2nd Division went through the smouldering ruins of Cité St. Edouard and Cité St. Laurent with equal ease. Both divisions reported themselves securely on their initial objective by twenty minutes after zero hour.

While the attackers paused to reorganize, shells began to fall among them, inflicting casualties. In the 16th (Canadian Scottish) Battalion's sector, Piper Alex McGillivray marched up and down playing his pipes and then stalked off to the left where the 13th Battalion (Royal Highlanders of Canada) were also consolidating. The 13th Battalion men saw the tall figure of the piper suddenly appear out of the smoke, his eyes blazing with excitement and his pipes shrilling. More than once it looked as though he must have been killed by some near shell-burst, but each time as the smoke cleared he was seen still upright and piping. Later, when McGillivray was on his way back to battalion headquarters where all pipers had to report after an assault, he disappeared, probably blown to pieces by a shell.

After a pause of twenty minutes, during which carrying parties brought up ammunition, bombs, and entrenching equipment, and stretcher-bearers began to evacuate the wounded, the Canadians moved forward again. On the right a defensive flank was established in Chicory Trench along the northern edge of Lens. The 20th (Central Ontario) Battalion captured its final objective, Commotion Trench, by 5.40 A.M., pushed out bombing and Lewis-gun posts, and sent patrols down two communication trenches, Nun's Alley and Nabob Alley. In the ruins of Cité Ste. Elisabeth sniper duels went on for some time before the last Germans were killed. In the centre, the 24th (Victoria Rifles) Battalion and the 26th (New Brunswick) Battalion took Cité St. Emile and Nun's Alley, and the 7th (British Columbia) Battalion and the 8th Battalion (90th Rifles), who had the farthest to go, reached their intermediate position, the Red Line. On the left the three Highland battalions of the 3rd Brigade, the 13th, 15th, and 16th, captured their final objective, Hugo Trench.

Hill 70 had changed hands for the last time in the war, and so far Canadian casualties had been gratifyingly light. But the worst still lay ahead. General Currie had been right in thinking the enemy would do his utmost to regain the lost ground.

One final phase of the operation still remained to be completed. In the centre, the 7th and 8th battalions were to advance a further 500 yards to capture Norman Trench and the Chalk Quarry north of Cité St. Auguste. By now it was broad daylight; the smoke screen from the burning oil drums had cleared, and the enemy had had time to reorganize.

100

The ground was badly torn by shellfire, with numerous craters eight to ten feet deep, and machine-gun fire slowed the attackers so that their barrage got hopelessly ahead of them. The 8th Battalion's attack withered away, but the 7th Battalion, having disposed of several machine-gun nests, pushed one company into the strongly defended Chalk Quarry. After capturing fifty haggard, wild-eyed prisoners, the British Columbians held out in the quarry until late afternoon. By nightfall, however, the two battalions, which had started the day with a total trench strength of about 1,300 men, were back at the Red Line. Between them they could muster no more than 200 exhausted soldiers.

While the 7th Battalion had been desperately fighting its way forward to the Chalk Quarry, and losing men with every yard gained, one of the unit's stretcher-bearers, 39-year-old Private Michael O'Rourke of Vancouver, had worked with a complete disregard for his own safety. Time and again O'Rourke crawled out in the open under heavy fire to apply dressings to wounded soldiers and give them what comfort he could. Three times that morning shells fell so near him that he was partially buried by the uptossed earth. Once, when he saw a blinded Canadian stumbling helplessly about in no-man's-land while the Germans sniped at him, O'Rourke leapt from his trench and guided the man to safety, careless of the bullets that whined around him. Twice more during the retirement to the Red Line he rescued wounded comrades under the heaviest shellfire. So long as there were men to be succoured O'Rourke worked tirelessly and without thought for himself. He kept it up for three whole days, saving many lives and providing an inspiring example for all who saw him. His Victoria Cross was one of the most popular awards ever granted a member of the Canadian Corps.

Elsewhere along the Canadian front casualties mounted as the enemy brought his guns to bear on the captured area. Four times between seven and eight o'clock German infantry massed to counterattack, but each time Canadian artillery officers, who had hurriedly dug themselves observation posts on the bare crest of Hill 70, spotted the enemy through their binoculars and spoke sharp orders into their field telephones or wireless sets, now being used by artillery observation officers for the first time. Seconds later, back at Bully Grenay and Maroc, along the Lens-Béthune road, or by the Double Crassier south of Loos, the guns answered the call, flights of shells screamed through the air, the earth would suddenly spout upwards in black, smoke-wreathed geysers, and the clustered grey figures would be hurled away like scattered toys. A German regiment marching up the Lens-Carvin road was caught four separate times in devastating artillery concentrations and all but annihilated. One counterattack force forming up in the Bois Dix-Huit was led by a German officer on a white horse. He drew involuntary exclamations of admiration from the watching Canadians as he continued to ride calmly up and down his line while the shells fell all around him. But courage was of no avail against high explosive, and a moment or two later horse and rider lay mangled and dead among the other huddled forms that dotted the shattered wood.

Nevertheless, before the day was over the eight German battalions originally holding the line were reinforced by seven more. In the early afternoon waves of enemy troops poured out of their trenches and advanced on Hill 70. Each wave was cut down by shellfire, machine guns, and rifles, until the dead lay like a horrible grey carpet on the ground. Currie noted in his diary: "Our gunners, machine-gunners and infantry never had such targets." A little later another counterattack, launched from Cité St. Auguste against the 2nd Brigade's front, met the same fate. Only on the extreme left did the enemy have a temporary success. Some Germans reached Chicory Trench and retook a portion of it, but after fierce hand-to-hand fighting with bomb and bayonet were driven out again by 6.40 P.M.

As darkness fell there came a lull in the fighting. The Canadians had captured almost all their objectives, and, although they had lost 1,056 dead, 2,432 wounded, and 39 taken prisoner, the enemy's losses, because of his futile counterattacks, were certainly much higher. In the forward trenches utterly weary soliders lay down on the cold earth to snatch what sleep they could. The wounded sobbed and moaned and cried piteously for water; signal linesmen, stretcher-bearers, and carrying parties toiled back and forth all night; and each man knew with a sort of numbed fatalism that on the morrow it would be all to do again.

The enemy made no serious counterattacks on the 16th, but at four o'clock in the afternoon the 2nd Brigade tried again to capture Norman Trench and the Chalk Quarry, this time using the 5th and 10th battalions. Although the Germans fought bitterly for every foot of the 500 yards between the Red Line and Norman Trench, both Canadian units were on their final objective shortly after five o'clock. In the Chalk Quarry, strewn with the previous day's German and Canadian dead, the 10th Battalion killed over 100 of the enemy and took 130 prisoners. Many of these were mere boys in their teens, and many were horribly wounded. They held bleeding hands to shattered faces, or lay with an arm or leg torn away or with a naked rib-bone sticking out through a torn tunic.

The 5th Battalion's two assault companies fought heroically in Norman Trench, capturing fifty prisoners and eight machine guns. But the price was high. By 5.30 the two companies, which had set out an hour and a half before with about 300 men, could muster fewer than ten soldiers between them, and their supply of Mills bombs and small arms ammunition was running out. The handful of survivors had no alternative but to fall back once more to the Red Line.

As darkness fell, the 10th Battalion was still hanging on to its gains, although both its flanks were in the air and parties of the enemy continually tried to infiltrate the Canadian position. All telephone wires back to battalion headquarters were cut and a German barrage was falling behind the Canadian front line. In the gathering twilight the enemy could be heard massing for a counterattack that could hardly fail to overrun the undermanned 10th Battalion position. Two company runners volunteered to go back through the barrage with a message calling for artillery support. One runner was killed almost as soon as he set out, but the other, nineteen-year-old Private Harry Brown of Gananoque, stumbled on among the falling shells. He had gone about half way when a shell burst close beside him, almost tearing off one of his arms, but young Brown picked himself up and went on. At last he reached the close support lines and found a dugout. He fell down the sandbag steps with a crash, but retained consciousness long enough to extend his remaining hand with the note clutched in it. "Important message!" he gasped out to the officer bending over him, then closed his eyes. He died a few hours later in the dressing station, but his comrades in the line knew he had got through. Just when it seemed they must be overwhelmed, Canadian shells began falling among the assembling counterattack force, breaking it up with heavy casualties. Private Brown was awarded the Victoria Cross posthumously, one of six granted to Canadians in this operation.

That night the Germans shelled the Canadian gun positions about Loos. Interspersed among the high explosive shells were others that sounded like duds but which were actually filled with the deadly new mustard gas, now being used against the Canadians for the first time. This gas burned whatever it touched, raised huge septic blisters on the skin, blinded the eyes, and ate away the lungs. The Canadian gunners, working frantically to bring down defensive fire for the infantry, at first put on their box respirators, but when they discovered that the misted eyepieces slowed their rate of fire they took them off again rather than fail their comrades in the line. The Canadian guns remained in action that night, but at dawn the next day, as relieved battalions marched back to Marzingarbe through the Loos Hollow, they were shocked to see long rows of half-naked gunners writhing in agony on the ground, choking and gasping for breath.

On the evening of the 17th the counterattacks began again, this time directed against the Chalk Quarry where the 4th Battalion now held the front. At 11.30 P.M. Canadian sentries, peering into the darkness, saw a long line of shadowy figures advancing towards them about 100 yards away. The warning cry echoed along the trench – "Here they come!" – and seconds later a slashing fire from Lewis guns and rifles cut the attackers down. Again, at 2.30 A.M. on the 18th, the enemy attacked, and again he was beaten off with heavy loss. One final attack just before dawn also withered away in no-man's-land.

Early that morning on the right flank a German force managed briefly to break into Chicory Trench, held by the 20th (Central Ontario) Battalion, but the assault was driven back. As the attackers retired, the 20th Battalion captured a number of prisoners. These had to remain in the Canadian trench all day because intense shelling made it impossible to escort them to the rear. The Ontario men bandaged the enemy wounded, gave them cigarettes, and were soon trying to carry on friendly conversations with them.

At the other end of the Canadian line, where the 2nd (East. Ontario) Battalion was holding out in the Bois Hugo, a tremendous artillery bombardment began just before dawn. At 4.45 A.M. waves of Germans started across no-man's-land, preceded by men carrying tanks and lengths of hose. Many were shot down but the remainder pressed bravely on until they were close to the Canadian line. Then streams of flame spurted from the nozzles of the hoses as the enemy sought to sweep the parapet with liquid fire. This was the first time *Flammenwerfer* had been used against Canadian troops, and they were not much impressed with them. At least two of the new weapons were captured in hand-to-hand fighting.

More troublesome were the German bombers who worked their way forward from shell hole to shell hole, tossing their light "egg-bombs" with great accuracy into Hugo Trench. Attack after attack was broken, but still the Germans pressed in. South of the Bois Hugo, where the 2nd Battalion's No. 3 Company fought under Major O. M. Learmonth of Quebec City, the battle raged for hours. At the age of 23, Learmonth was already a veteran company commander, and that day as he stood on the parapet, blood dripping down his tunic from a wound, his bare flaxen head was a rallying point for his men. Several times when the little black German bombs were lobbed over near him he stretched out a long arm as though on the baseball field, caught the grenade, and hurled it back again. He was wounded a second time but fought on. When he was hit a third time and his leg broken he refused to leave the position and lay in the bottom of the trench directing the fight until the enemy had been beaten off. On his way back to the dressing station, although he was obviously dying, Learmonth insisted on stopping at battalion headquarters to make a complete report. He was awarded a posthumous Victoria Cross.

When the enemy failed in his final attempt to retake the

Chalk Quarry, the Canadian front grew quiet. After four days and three nights of bitter fighting there was a lull. Currie confided to his diary: "It was altogether the hardest battle in which the Corps has participated. There were no fewer than twenty-one counterattacks delivered, many with very large forces and all with great determination and dash."

However, the hope that the fighting at Hill 70 would distract the enemy from the great offensive in Flanders was not to be realized. General Ludendorff had visited the Lens sector on the 18th, but after listening coldly to reports and studying the map through his monocle, he arrived at the correct conclusion — the principal British effort would not be here but in Flanders.

It would have been better if the battle had ended then, with the principal objectives won, the enemy counterattacks beaten off, and the captured ground consolidated. Instead, because the higher command was still obsessed with the idea of taking the town of Lens, the Canadians launched a series of new attacks. North of Lens the 6th Brigade was to capture a small rectangle of ground crisscrossed with a maze of trenches like a rabbit warren and bounded by Nun's Alley, Cinnabar Trench, and Combat Trench. West of Lens the 10th Brigade of Major-General D. Watson's 4th Division was to drive into the town itself towards the Arras road. These attacks resulted in very fierce but inconclusive fighting, in which trenches, slag heaps, and ruined hamlets changed hands again and again.

Both assaults went in simultaneously just before dawn on August 21. On the left of the 6th Brigade's front, when the 29th Battalion advanced in the darkness across open fields, it ran headlong into a German guards battalion coming across no-man's-land in the opposite direction. What followed was surely one of the strangest fights in history. The German barrage fell behind the Canadians and the Canadian barrage behind the Germans, isolating both groups and leaving them for the moment on a fantastic twilight stage of their own. The early light was almost too faint for men to distinguish field-grey from khaki. Friend could best be told from foe by the silhouette of coal-scuttle helmet or round tin hat, by the cut of uniforms, and by the language used to swear in. The lines locked in combat; bayonets stabbed; rifle butts swung; less frequently shots were fired. Both barrages passed on, receding on either side like tides going out, but the struggling soldiers had scarcely time to notice this. Men fell and others stepped over them to take their place. Finally the Germans began to give ground, slowly at first and then more rapidly, as happens in the last few seconds of a tug-of-war match. Then the enemy broke and fled, leaving the Vancouver men to make their way forward to Nun's Alley.

Not all of the 29th Battalion's objectives were captured, however, and elsewhere, too, success was only partial. Late in the afternoon both the 27th and 29th battalions retired to their original positions.

On the 10th Brigade front west of Lens the 50th Battalion was heavily shelled while forming up, suffered more than a hundred casualties, and had to change assault companies. In no-man's-land the Calgary men were so badly raked by machine-gun and artillery fire that only a handful reached their objective at the junction of the Béthune and La Bassée roads. Although the 46th Battalion also lost many officers and men, it captured all its objectives. By nightfall, the 47th Battalion, too, reported success, after having spent all day grimly fighting its way through the ruined suburbs of Lens and losing many men to German machine guns concealed in the rubble and shell holes.

During the next two days further attacks by the 4th Division failed to make appreciable progress, but on August 22 the 44th Battalion was ordered to make a night assault on the Green Crassier, a strongly fortified slag heap some 350 yards ahead of the new front line. After a personal reconnaissance, the battalion commander strongly advised that the operation be cancelled. He pointed out that as soon as daylight came any Canadians on the Crassier would be hopelessly isolated and that the Fosse St. Louis, a cluster of ruined pithead buildings dominating the objective, was swarming with Germans. These protests were ignored. The attack went in as ordered, and everything the battalion commander had predicted came to pass. The 44th Battalion lost 257 men and the Green Crassier remained in German hands until just before the armistice in 1918. On August 25 the 50th Battalion launched one final attack which gained all the objectives it had been given four days previously.

With this the battle finally died down. Between August 15 and August 25 the fighting around Hill 70 had cost the Canadian Corps 9,198 casualties, about one-third of which were fatal. German losses were certainly much higher. Considerable ground had been gained, and sixteen Canadian battalions had decisively defeated twenty-one German battalions drawn from five divisions. As had happened after the capture of Vimy Ridge, this battle had been persisted in too long, with the result that as the defence stiffened Canadian casualties mounted out of all proportion to the gains made. The error is perhaps significant as exemplifying a state of mind. On the German side, it was, as it turned out, a mistake to launch immediate, uncoordinated counterattacks which could be broken up piecemeal, although it is very doubtful whether a deliberate counterattack on a large scale would have been any more successful. In retrospect a phrase of Currie's stands out as the most significant comment upon the battle: "If," he had said to Horne, "we have to fight at all – "

Whether the cost of Hill 70 had been worth while would depend on the result of Haig's cherished Flanders offensive – and the Canadians were to have first-hand experience of that operation all too soon.

A cold rain drizzled down from the grey October sky and patches of ground mist swirled above the cobbles as the Canadian infantrymen marched out of Ypres station. They looked hunchbacked and misshapen under their packs and rolled blankets, and their damp greatcoats all seemed a little too large for them. The few remaining veterans of 1915 could scarcely recognize the town they had known. The battered ruins of St. Martin's Cathedral and the Cloth Hall were still standing, but almost everything else was rubble. On their way through Ypres the Canadians passed Australian troops going in the opposite direction. Most were white-faced and silent, but some called out to the newcomers, and what they had to say was not reassuring.

For five days, between October 16 and October 20, 1917, battalion after battalion of Canadian soldiers tumbled out of the little French railway boxcars marked "Hommes 40, Chevaux 8", formed up in Ypres station yard, and moved off in column of route beneath sodden skies. They no longer sang on the march, but their feet pounded out a monotonous rhythm as they tramped through the broken arch of the Menin Gate, crossed the footbridge over the Yser Canal, and headed northeast along the road to Potijze and the line. In the previous three months perhaps a million men had passed through that fatal gate on the same frightful journey.

Outside Ypres the Canadians came upon a dreary plain,

stretching as far as the eye could see. None of the old land-marks any longer existed – Wieltje, St. Jean, St. Julien, For-tuin, remembered farmhouses, barns, and *estaminets* had all disappeared without a trace. What the soldiers saw was a landscape out of a nightmare, a grey, evil-smelling waste of stagnant, scum-coated water and mud. Across this expanse of blurred desolation they could just make out the low, misty outline of Passchendaele ridge some two miles ahead.

Conversation died in the ranks as the men stared incredu-lously. Could this seriously be intended as a battleground? It seemed completely featureless, without a scrap of vegetation; it was nothing but a vast swamp. The road forward was of planks, laid on fascines to prevent it from sinking into the morass. Before long even this came to an end and the soldiers went over wooden duckboards greasy with mud. Every so often a gap in the duckboards showed where a shell had landed, and then the men had to plunge up past their knees into the clinging slime.

On close inspection, the area was not quite featureless. Thousands of shell holes dotted this fantastic plain, and some were unforgettable. All were filled with water, but in some the water was reddened with blood, and in some there floated horribly bloated corpses. Sometimes only an arm or leg was visible, poking out of the scum; sometimes a blackened, swollen face, scarcely recognizable as human, gazed up vacantly at the rainy sky. The stench of death and corruption caught at the throat and turned the stomach. It was danger-ously easy to slip off the duckboard. In the days and nights ahead many men were to die that way, sinking down help-lessly and suffocating as their mouths and nostrils clogged with the stinking Salient mud. Horses and mules were often swallowed up by the swamp; so were guns, vehicles, and long stretches of light railway track.

Before taking their places in the trenches most units bivouacked in the open, for the few small dugouts were water-logged. The soldiers improvised what cover they could with their ground-sheets and with the stray sheets of corrugated iron that littered the ground, but nothing could keep out the incessant rain.

The entire Salient was under constant shellfire, and since it was crowded with troops the German gunners could scarcely fail to hit something whenever they brought down a bombardment. The only good thing about the mud was that shells tended to bury themselves in it before exploding, thus losing much of their effectiveness. At night the enemy's new Gotha aeroplanes droned over to drop random bombs. Occasionally, dressing stations filled with wounded were hit, and there were some horrible scenes when horse lines were shelled.

This was the battlefield of Passchendaele when the Canadians arrived to play their heroic part in the futile tragedy being enacted there.

A month later, when the battle was over, Lieutenant-General Sir Launcelot Kiggell, chief of staff to Field Marshal Sir Douglas Haig, made his first visit to the former forward zone. He drove out through the Menin Gate comfortably in a staff car, but as he approached the old battlefield he became more and more agitated. At last he burst into tears and exclaimed: "Good God, did we really send men to fight in that?" The combatant officer who accompanied him replied shortly: "It's worse farther up."

In fact, they sent men to fight "in that" for the better part of four months. Except for three weeks of dry weather in September, when the British had been too busy regrouping to attack, the battleground had been "a porridge of mud" ever since the offensive had started on July 31. Haig's staff should not have been surprised, for before the campaign began they had carefully studied the weather records of the previous eighty years and learned that "the weather broke early each August with the regularity of the Indian monsoon". They had been warned, too, that this section of Flanders was land reclaimed from the sea, artificially drained and kept above water only by an elaborate system of dikes and ditches. They had been warned that artillery bombardment would destroy this drainage system, that the clay soil was impervious and would not absorb moisture. They had, in short, been warned most explicitly of what would happen. What they had not done was look at the battlefield themselves.

For more than a year and a half Sir Douglas Haig had dreamed of a great Flanders offensive in which the British armies under his command would win the war single-handed.

111

He had chosen to attack in the Ypres Salient because there "success seemed reasonably certain", because even if "a full measure of success is not gained . . . our purpose of wearing down [the enemy] will be given effect to", and because to break out of the Salient would "reduce the heavy wastage which must occur there next winter as in the past, if our troops hold the same positions". Haig rejected the simple expedient of withdrawing from the deathtrap of the Salient and thereby shortening and strengthening the British line. The previous year he had been outraged when "some pluckless Canadians" had advocated such a course.

Before Haig attacked, every one of his army commanders had expressed strong reservations about his plan. Prime Minister Lloyd George, Winston Churchill, and other cabinet ministers thought the scheme senseless and feared it would result in another bloodbath like the Somme. General Foch said that Haig's proposed "duck's march through the inundations to Ostend and Zeebrugge" was "futile, fantastic, and dangerous". But the Commander-in-Chief, with the calm unconcern of a sleepwalker, persisted in his course.

In June he promised the Cabinet War Committee that the French would co-operate fully in his attack, although he knew full well that fifty-four French divisions had just mutinied because of the bloody failure of Nivelle's Champagne offensive. He assured the War Committee that the Germans were demoralized, that he could capture the entire Flemish coast and win the war, and that if he did not achieve a significant initial success he would at once break off the attack rather than pile up needless casualties.

Lloyd George and Churchill were completely unconvinced by any of this. Not even the demand of Admiral Jellicoe, the First Sea Lord, that the German submarine bases on the Belgian coast be captured made them change their minds. Haig used Jellicoe to support his arguments for an offensive, although he admitted privately that he did not agree with the admiral's assessment. Lloyd George and Churchill would infinitely have preferred to reinforce the dangerously weak Italian front and to have stood on the defensive in France and Flanders until fresh American troops arrived, but the War Committee did not see fit to overrule the Commander-

The battlefield at Passchendaele, November 1917

German troops surrendering at Vimy Ridge, April 1917

Passchendaele – a sea of mud

Canadian and German wounded help one another through the mud at Passchendaele.

Canadian heavy artillerymen manoeuvring a howitzer into position, December 1917

Canadian artillery observation post, January 1918

in-Chief. This, it should be noted, was not because the politicians had confidence in him or his plan but because they could not summon up the courage to replace him. In July Haig had been given formal permission to launch his offensive.

Haig's plan called for General Gough's Fifth Army to attack the eastern side of the Salient, advance fifteen miles in the first eight days, and capture the whole loop of the Ypres-Roulers-Thourout railway. Rawlinson's Fourth Army would then make an amphibious landing south of Ostend, and Gough and Rawlinson together would sweep up the coast and turn the German right flank. Haig believed there would be fine "opportunities for the employment of cavalry in masses".

In the first four weeks of the Passchendaele campaign, officially known as the Third Battle of Ypres, the British lost 68,000 men for an average advance of less than two miles along a few thousand yards of front, and the amphibious landings had to be abandoned. How any other result could rationally have been predicted in the light of all past experience on the Western Front is impossible to imagine. Nevertheless, the offensive was continued and the entire British army was combed for men and artillery to sustain the attack. When the Canadian Corps was thrown into the Passchendaele swamp, all but nine of the sixty British divisions had been committed in the Salient. Haig no longer spoke of taking Ostend and Zeebrugge, of brilliant cavalry charges, of rolling up the German flank and winning the war. Instead his eyes were now fixed hypnotically on a few small map squares of worthless mud. He evaded his promise to discontinue the offensive if substantial initial success was not achieved by the simple expedient of claiming that substantial success *had* been achieved – although by the end of October, after three months of bloody fighting, objectives that were to have been captured on the first day were still untaken. This same technique of deliberate falsehood had worked well at the Somme. It was assisted by a clique of politicians in England who felt that criticism of generals was unpatriotic, by military secrecy that made the facts hard to come by, and by the ready gullibility of a public anxious to believe the best.

The front-line soldiers were not deceived. General Sir

Arthur Currie had wanted no part of Passchendaele. No sensible soldier could help being appalled by the prospect of fighting there, and Currie was eminently sensible. He had made a personal appeal to Haig not to send the Canadians to the Salient. "I carried my protest to the extreme limit," Currie later wrote, ". . . which I believe would have resulted in my being sent home had I been other than the Canadian Corps Commander. I pointed out what the casualties were bound to be, and asked if a success would justify the sacrifice. I was ordered to go and make the attack."

Since Haig had berated General Alderson in the Canadian Division's headquarters near Festubert two and a half years before, only the Commander-in-Chief's manners had improved. He was still issuing the same kind of orders.

At the time, Haig had declined to give Currie any reason for his stubborn stand, merely saying: "Some day I will tell you why, but Passchendaele must be taken." After the war Haig told Currie that to "help the morale of the French army and of the French people and the British people, he was determined to finish the fighting of 1917 with a victory" – an explanation, it should be noted, widely at variance with the reasons he had given the British War Cabinet.*

At least Currie was successful in his insistence that, if the Canadians had to fight at Passchendaele, they would fight as a united corps or not at all. Another point he was able to carry was that the Canadians would not serve in Gough's Fifth Army. Like Haig, Gough was a cavalryman and Haig admired his "cavalry spirit", but he had a bad reputation with the fighting troops. When the Canadians had been under him at the Somme, complaints about his staff work had been bitter. It is said that when Currie refused to risk Canadian lives under Gough, Haig replied: "Currie, do you realize this is in-

* In the Second World War care was taken that this sort of situation could not happen again. When General A. G. L. McNaughton was commander of the Canadian Army Overseas he was specifically given the right of reference to the Canadian government and was authorized, in an extreme emergency, to withdraw Canadian forces from their role of acting "in combination with" the British. McNaughton, who had been an artillery brigadier in the First World War, vividly remembered Currie's difficulties.

subordination?" And Currie answered: "Yes sir, but I cannot help that." At all events, the Canadian Corps was placed in General Plumer's Second Army.

Currie also extracted a promise from Haig that the Canadians would not have to attack before their preparations were complete. It was well that he did so, for when his artillery commander, Brigadier-General Morrison, took over his allotted guns from the Australians, he could find only 227 of the 250 heavy pieces he was supposed to have, and of these 89 were out of action; of 306 field guns, fewer than half were serviceable. Moreover, the guns were very badly sited, since moving them was so difficult; often they had slipped off the makeshift roads and disappeared completely in the mud. However, by intelligent staff work and tremendous exertions the artillery was regrouped, brought up to strength, and was ready for action by October 26.

Two days before the first Canadian attack, the Austrians, aided by six German divisions, struck on the Italian front at Caporetto and all but knocked Italy out of the war. Italian formations streamed rearward in panic, and before long Italy had lost, in dead, wounded, prisoners, and deserters, some 800,000 soldiers.

At Passchendaele, quite apart from the natural obstacles imposed by the condition of the battle area, the Canadians would have to crack formidable defences. In June, Colonel von Lossberg, the great defensive expert, had become chief of staff to the German Fourth Army in Flanders. He had at once introduced a new type of defence in depth in which a battle zone replaced rigid trench lines, dugouts, and barbed-wire entanglements. Lossberg planned to hold his front with minimum manpower and maximum firepower, so in place of a continuous trench line he built a checkerboard pattern of reinforced concrete pillboxes that bristled with machine guns – that "concentrated essence of infantry". Most shells bounced off these strong-points "like tennis balls off a sidewalk", and the garrisons of the pillboxes were the only men on all that battlefield who fought in relative comfort and safety from artillery fire. This concept of area, rather than linear, defence meant that more ground could be held by

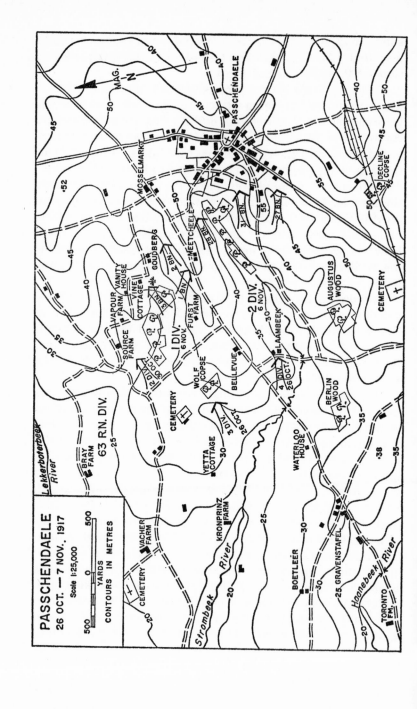

PASSCHENDAELE
26 OCT. — 7 NOV., 1917

Scale 1:25,000

YARDS

CONTOURS IN METRES

fewer men. It gave desirable depth to the defence, made the attacker's artillery tasks much more difficult, and facilitated mutual fire support.

Currie planned three separate attacks, the first of which would be launched at dawn on October 26. Because the flooded Ravesbeek stream formed an impassable swamp in the centre of the battlefield, the initial assault had to be split in two, with the 3rd Division advancing north of the morass and the 4th Division making a separate attack to the south.

Drinking water was scarce on that water-logged plain, for the liquid that filled the shell holes was contaminated with the death and refuse of a civilization. With infinite labour and at the risk of their lives, carrying parties brought water up to the line in petrol tins. As a result it always had a lingering taste of petrol, but it was precious for all that. On the night before the attack some carrying parties went astray, and the 4th C.M.R.s at least had to go into battle in the morning with empty water bottles.

The troops were all assembled by four o'clock, and sharp at 5.40 A.M., as the second hands of hundreds of synchronized wristwatches climbed up to the minute mark, 210 eighteen-pounders, 190 howitzers, and 26 heavy guns opened fire together. Because of the condition of the battlefield the barrage advanced slowly in lifts of fifty yards every four minutes, or less than half a mile an hour. As the attackers moved forward they waded up to their knees, and sometimes up to their waists, in mud. Shortly after daybreak the icy wind blew up a steady rain that lasted all day.

South of the Ravesbeek, the 46th Battalion cleared Decline Copse of its Bavarian defenders, and although the enemy later infiltrated back again, the 44th Battalion recaptured the lost ground. Farther north the fighting was sharper as the Cameron Highlanders of Canada and the 58th Battalion struggled forward in the face of sweeping machine-gun fire, but by nine o'clock both units had reached the Bellevue Spur. Here, however, they came under artillery fire so murderous that the survivors fell back to their start line. Only on the left centre, where a party of Camerons had a few pillboxes, were Canadian gains retained.

On the extreme left the advance went better, although the

117

cost was terribly high. The 4th C.M.R.s took Wolfe Copse and reached their intermediate objective, but had to retire some 300 yards and form a defensive flank when the 63rd (Royal Naval) Division to the north failed to keep pace. In this single day's fighting the 4th C.M.R.s lost 17 out of 21 officers and 304 other ranks. At noon the 52nd (Lake Superior) Battalion established contact with the gallant little group on Bellevue Spur. The men from the Lakehead retook the spur, then turned and worked their way south through the mire to the fortified hamlet of Laamkeek. They stalked and overcame pillbox after pillbox, taking more than 100 prisoners.

All this while the rain had poured down incessantly from a pewter-coloured sky. Consolidation meant taking up positions along the rim of water-filled shell holes and in captured pillboxes. Machine guns and rifles clogged with mud and had to be cleaned again and again. The task of bringing up ammunition, water, and rations was heartbreakingly difficult, for only mules and men could move at all in the forward areas and even these often bogged down hopelessly. Later in the afternoon, when the Royal Flying Corps sent contact aircraft over the battlefield to report the positions of the foremost Canadian troops, the soldiers had to signal by standing up and waving their steel helmets in the air, since their flares were all too wet to light.

On the 4th C.M.R.s' front, the unit chaplain, Captain W. H. Davis, courageously led stretcher-bearer parties about the battlefield. A few hundred yards away, the Germans watched this without opening fire, and then – timidly at first but later with growing confidence – they emerged to tend the wounded in their own area. When they came on a wounded Canadian, they either carried him to the shelter of a pillbox or marked his position by sticking his rifle into the mud and placing his steel helmet on top of it. Before long Canadian and German stretcher-bearers were mingling on the field and meeting in pillboxes to exchange wounded men. The unofficial truce lasted some two hours, but as evening began to close miserably in some young Canadian artillery officer, unable to resist the target presented by so many enemy in the open, brought down fire that drove everyone to cover.

On other portions of the front, when darkness gave some

protection from enemy fire, the walking wounded set out through the mud to advanced dressing stations in the rear. Many never completed the journey. Some slipped into mud holes and suffocated; some drowned in the flooded Ravesbeek; and not a few died of exhaustion on the way. The first phase of operations ended with the line advanced 800 yards, although the final objectives on the left had not been taken. Between October 26 and October 29 the Canadians lost 2,481 men, about one-third of whom had been killed.

Before the second Canadian attack, on October 30, the six assaulting battalions assembled under a bright moon that washed the muddy ground with silver light and made glinting mirrors of the myriad, water-filled craters. The night was cold with the chill of late autumn and the soldiers shivered as they waited for zero hour. At such times they were apt to think longingly of half-forgotten things – warm rooms, clean beds, firelight, the smell of coffee wafting up from the kitchen in the morning at home. Perhaps the war would really go on forever, or until everyone on both sides was dead. Such possibilities did not seem absurd as the soldiers looked out at the mud they were to capture in the morning. At two o'clock the moon went down and the sky darkened, but it was not until 5.50 A.M. that the barrage crashed out and the infantry went forward to their day's work.

On the right, the 85th Battalion (Nova Scotia Highlanders), the 78th Battalion (Winnipeg Grenadiers), and the 72nd Battalion (Seaforth Highlanders of Canada) took Vienna Cottage and Crest Farm and reached all their objectives by 8.30. As they consolidated, the Germans began a bombardment that lasted all day. On the left, Princess Patricia's Canadian Light Infantry took the pillboxes known as Snipe Hall and Duck Lodge and then pressed on to clear the hamlet of Meetcheele, but was stopped about halfway to its objective. On the extreme left the 5th Canadian Mounted Rifles captured Source Farm and Vapour Farm, drove the enemy out of the swamp known as Woodland Plantation, and consolidated on their final objective. Late in the afternoon General Currie ordered the Canadians to stop and consolidate, although not all objectives had been captured. The line had been advanced about 1,000 yards along a 2,800-yard front, for a cost of 884 Canadian dead and 1,429 wounded.

The 3rd and 4th divisions were now replaced by the 1st and 2nd divisions, and the battle continued. Although the objectives of the third phase included the village of Passchendaele and the hamlets of Mosselmarkt and Goudberg, by no conceivable military standard could this area be considered vital ground. But as Currie later said: "Passchendaele seemed to symbolize [to Haig] all the difficulties; and he chose for its capture the only corps in France capable of doing it. That is why the Canadians went to Passchendaele."

The attack went in at six o'clock in the morning of November 6 from a jumping-off line that was nearly half under water. On the left the 1st (Ontario) and the 2nd (East Ontario) battalions had little difficulty, but the 3rd Battalion (The Toronto Regiment) had to fight bitterly to capture the enemy stronghold known as Vine Cottage.

The 28th (North West), the 31st (Alberta), and the 27th (City of Winnipeg) battalions attacked towards the village of Passchendaele itself. The 28th Battalion men had to wade through icy, waist-deep water to come to grips with the German machine-gunners opposite them, but by nine o'clock they were securely on their objective. Although the day was overcast with heavy clouds that continually threatened rain, low-flying German aircraft frequently strafed the advancing Canadians. Before the attack the men of the 31st Battalion had been ordered to remove their greatcoats and leave them on the start line, an order that had been greeted with a good deal of grumbling since the weather was bitterly cold. A few hours later when carrying parties brought up the greatcoats, the Alberta men found many of them riddled with bullets, for a German aircraft had mistaken the row of coats for soldiers and had thoroughly machine-gunned them.

In Passchendaele village many German defenders had been wounded by the Canadian barrage, but they fought on bravely, their faces deathly white from loss of blood and their heads and arms often swathed in bloodstained bandages. They clung grimly to their positions in cellars, ruined houses, pillboxes, and shell holes, manning their machine guns to the last moment, and had to be rooted out in dozens of little engagements.

Even now the long-drawn-out battle was not over. The Canadians were ordered to attack once more and capture the remaining high ground north of the village. On November 10, a day of pouring rain, the 8th Battalion (90th Rifles), the 7th (British Columbia) Battalion, and the 20th (Central Ontario) Battalion wearily slogged forward against indifferent German resistance and did what they had been sent to do.

The enemy, having a true appreciation of the value of the ground, did not bother to counterattack. However, the captured area was saturated with intense shellfire, and enemy aircraft enthusiastically machine-gunned the line of muddy shell holes that was the Canadian front. The fighting on November 10 cost 1,094 casualties, 420 of them fatal.

On November 15 Haig finally called a halt. In spite of his protests he had had to send five divisions to bolster the Italian front, and the French were insisting that he take over more trench line. The offensive had lasted 109 days. During that time the Ypres Salient had been deepened by four and a half miles.

As with the Somme, there is still doubt about comparative casualty figures – and for the same discreditable reasons. Probably the forces under Haig's command lost some 300,-000 men in the Passchendaele offensive, since total British casualties for the last six months of 1917 were 448,614. During the same period, the Germans lost 270,710 on the entire Western Front including the much longer stretch where they faced French and Belgian armies. Canadian losses were accurately computed; they totalled 15,654 men.

Five days after Haig stopped his offensive, Sir Julian Byng's Third Army, without any preliminary bombardment, launched a surprise attack with massed tanks at Cambrai. On the first day Byng drove forward four miles on a six-mile front, stormed through the immensely strong Hindenburg Line, and captured thousands of prisoners and many guns. British losses for this signal victory were slightly under 4,000. Since the reserves that might have been used to exploit success had been dissipated at Passchendaele, nothing came of it all except a striking lesson for history.

Thus at the end of 1917 the outlook for the Allies was bleak. Propaganda made the most of Allenby's triumphal entry into Jerusalem in December, but thoughtful men knew that such far-flung victories would have little effect upon the ultimate course of the war. The new Bolshevik government in Russia signed an armistice with Germany at Brest-Litovsk on December 18 and German divisions and corps began to be shipped from the Eastern Front to the Western Front. The longed-for American forces, who would eventually redress the balance, were still not ready for battle, and only a few American divisions would be in Europe before midsummer of 1918. Most serious of all, the British army had been severely weakened, and more than a little shaken, by the futile Flanders fighting.

The Canadians had been magnificent at Passchendaele. Under indescribable conditions and for objectives whose selection seemed insane, they had fought intelligently and with high courage. But, being thinking creatures, they continually asked themselves why. Even today the question has no satisfactory answer. Haig later claimed that he persisted "to help the French", but as early as October 11 the French President, M. Poincaré, had asked him to stop the attack and take over more line. Haig's defenders have spread the story that General Pétain "implored" Haig to continue his offensive. This is untrue. The only record of a comment by Pétain on the operation is a letter he wrote to Haig on June 30, in which he said: ". . . l'offensive des Flandres doit être assurée d'un succès absolu, impérieusement exigé par les facteurs moraux du moment." By an amazing inversion, the apologists for Haig claim that this shows Pétain pressing for the Flanders offensive, expressing certainty of success, and claiming that it was necessary to restore French morale. Of course, what Pétain was actually doing was telling Haig that, if he was indeed going to launch an offensive, he had better make very sure he succeeded because Allied morale could not stand another disaster such as had recently occurred in Champagne. Pétain knew by sad experience what could happen to an army that was callously and incompetently handled.

Then what was the reason for it all? Lloyd George later spoke of "individuals who would rather the million perish than that they as leaders should own — even to themselves —

that they were blunderers". He also castigated Haig's staff: "The whole atmosphere of this secluded little community reeked of that sycophantic optimism which is the curse of autocratic power." Fifty years later these stern judgments still have the unmistakable ring of truth, and their truth is in no way diminished, although it is indeed made more poignant and ironical, by the *tu quoque* that Lloyd George, knowing beforehand the manner of men with whom he was dealing, did not risk his political career to thwart their stupidities. Certainly, in 1918, when Haig knew that the British government and people were at long last running out of patience and after his chief of intelligence, Brigadier-General Charteris, and his chief of staff, General Kiggell, were replaced, British strategy was more sensible.

In any case, Canada could take pride in the achievements of her soldiers at Passchendaele. But it was a pride tempered by the remembrance of horror and shadowed by sorrow for all the valour that had been wilfully poured out into the ground.

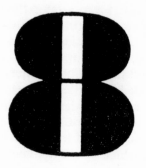

While the Canadian Corps in France was being tempered by battle, unified by common hardship and danger, and sublimated by sacrifice, the effects of the war in Canada were almost exactly the opposite. The losses of 1916 and 1917 shocked the Canadian people. As day after day the newspapers came out with their black-bordered casualty columns, the Canadian mood changed. Tension, fear, sorrow, and a sort of stunned determination to see it through replaced the flamboyant pride of Empire that had been characteristic of 1914. For the first time, too, there began to be doubts – about the conduct of the war if not about its necessity.

For some sections of the Canadian public, however, the war was proving highly advantageous. The purchase of Victory Bonds, which paid a minimum of five per cent interest and were tax free forever, enabled financiers, insurance companies, and banks, who were the principal subscribers, to combine profit with patriotism. Farmers, industrialists, and organized labour also prospered under war conditions.

With tens of millions of workers and farmers in uniform, with industry diverted to armament production, with shipping losses and the destruction of industrial capacity in the war zones, serious world shortages inevitably developed. By far the gravest of these was the food shortage. Both belligerent groups were forced to institute severe rationing, and in Russia, in the Balkans, and even in Germany and Austria there was actual starvation. The diversion of shipping to war purposes also helped create famines in Asia and the Middle East.

Canada, still primarily an agricultural country, profited from these conditions. The price of No. 1 Northern wheat tripled as it climbed to over two dollars a bushel. Cheese exports increased by 300 per cent, pork exports by 535 per cent, and beef exports by 6,795 per cent. Canada's wheat acreage doubled; wheat production soared to about 450 million bushels a year. Little thought was given to soil conservation, economic work methods, or care of equipment.

Canadian industry was much slower to benefit from the war. British manufacturers, with an eye on post-war competition, were initially reluctant to have orders placed outside the United Kingdom, and in 1914 and early 1915 Canadian agents were repeatedly told that Britain had enough shells on hand to last for the duration of hostilities. Russia ordered five million howitzer shells from the Canadian Car and Foundry Company, and the Nova Scotia Steel and Coal Company received a small order for casings, but until a new British Department of Munitions and Supply was created in the late spring of 1915 Canada produced little war material.

In the summer of 1915, an Imperial Munitions Board under Joseph Flavelle, a Toronto businessman, was established, and thereafter Canadian industry prospered almost as much as Canadian agriculture. By the end of the war 1,500 factories in ninety Canadian cities employed 350,000 men and women in war production. Canada began to build her own refineries for processing metal ore, partly because of the fear that Canadian ore shipped to the neutral United States for processing might find its way to Germany. Canadian secondary industry more than doubled between 1914 and 1918, but its production was highly specialized and the increased output was not accompanied by any corresponding increase in the size of population or in potential post-war markets.

This great bonanza was marked by a series of scandals, by hugely inflated war profits, and by a sharp delineation of opposing interest on the part of capital and labour. No serious attempt was made to curtail profits or increase taxation. An income tax was introduced in 1916, as was a business profits tax, but both these were the mildest of measures, intended, as the finance minister, Sir Thomas White, admitted, "not to hamper industry or breed discontent among the people". War taxes brought the Canadian government only about $50 million a year.

In 1915, when it became apparent that the Canadian army had been sold 180,000 pairs of almost useless boots, there was a public outcry and investigation. Of the first 8,500 horses purchased by the army one in four was unfit for service; some had been rejected in the Boer War. Charges of profiteering in drugs, bandages, optical instruments, and foodstuffs were made and substantiated, and Sir Robert Borden, much embarrassed, forced the resignation of two Conservative Members of Parliament for participating in some of these ventures.

Meanwhile, Minister of Militia Sam Hughes had created a Shell Committee, staffed with honorary colonels who were his personal friends, to be responsible for the purchase of war supplies. The country was dismayed, but not unduly surprised, to learn that Honorary Colonel J. Wesley Allison, an old friend of Hughes, had accepted a personal gratuity of $220,000 from the American Ammunition Company in return for ensuring that the Shell Committee would place a $10 million order for artillery fuses with the firm. Since the American Ammunition Company had no plant and no capital, the Shell Committee had obligingly advanced $1,500,000 so that the firm could begin operations. It was also discovered that members of the Shell Committee had made money on munitions contracts, that contracts were often let without competitive bidding, and that large orders had been placed in the United States when they could have been filled in Canada.

Borden was reluctant to take action against Hughes because he believed, rightly or wrongly, that Hughes controlled a large bloc of Orange votes and that the loss of this political support might endanger his administration. Unrepentant and blustering, Hughes defended his friend Allison in the House of Commons, blamed the Auditor General for making "reflections on a gentleman who has more honour in his little finger than the Auditor General has in his whole carcass", and threatened to find a way to make the Auditor General pay for his presumption. When Borden was at last forced to appoint a royal commission, it placed the blame on Colonel Allison and exonerated Hughes, although its report rather inconsistently noted that the Minister of Militia had influenced the Shell Committee to award contracts to his constituents, including his own son-in-law.

Other unpleasant results of the war were also becoming evident in Canada. Press and pulpit were used to disseminate a spurious patriotism that was often no more than a gospel of hate. Young women were encouraged to present white feathers to young men who were not in uniform. The name of the old Ontario town of Berlin was changed in 1916 to Kitchener. It became unpatriotic to own a dachshund or enjoy Beethoven.

But none of this, fortunately, was truly representative of Canada at war. In hundreds of thousands of homes across the Dominion the near relatives and friends of the soldiers serving overseas carried on from day to day, proud of their men, deeply anxious for the future, waking each morning to the fear that this might be the day when the doorbell would ring and the dreaded official telegram arrive – "The Department of Militia and Defence deeply regrets to inform you . . ." Often their fears were confirmed, and sometimes more than once. It was a time for prayer, for tension in the waking hours, for tears at night – a time for regrets and a time for fortitude. Knitting for the soldiers at the front was a kind of therapy, even when the pattern blurred and the futility of the stitching struck at the heart. Some of the very badly wounded came home to walk about the familiar, maple-lined streets in khaki or hospital-blue, their empty sleeves pinned across their tunics and strange knowledge in their eyes.

It was a time for all those things, but it was not yet a time for reassessment, for cold analysis of causes and results, for seeing men and events in a clear, hard light. There was, as was commonly said, a war on. And while there was a war, objectivity could too easily be made to look like disloyalty, criticism like treason. Nevertheless, more than the Canadian mood had changed, although during the war itself this change generally manifested itself by no more than a vague sense of unease, a reluctant doubt that Allied generalship was infallible, and a growing revulsion among the thoughtful at the facile slogans of the super-patriots at home.

Throughout 1914 and 1915 recruiting had been satisfactory. Medical standards had been relaxed in 1915, and the regulation that had required a married man to produce the written consent of his wife before he could be enrolled was cancelled. Recruiting depots had been established in most cities and larger towns, and Citizens Recruiting Leagues and Committees had been formed to organize rallies, raise funds, and stimulate enthusiasm.

When in June 1915 the War Office had requested that Canada provide a third division, the Prime Minister and Major-General W. G. Gwatkin, the Chief of the General Staff, had doubts as to whether this would not be an excessive demand on Canada's manpower. Nevertheless, by November 1915 the recruiting situation seemed so favourable that the Deputy Minister of Militia, Major-General Sir Eugène Fiset, wrote the Under-Secretary of State for External Affairs: "So whole-hearted has been the response . . . that the equivalent of a Division [the third] can be added, without difficulty, to the Canadian Army Corps already in the trenches." This was in marked contrast to his opinion in July when he had advised that the maintenance of the two divisions, the cavalry brigade, and other troops overseas was "as much as Canada should undertake". The new division was formed by the end of 1915, and in December, after discussion with the War Office, a fourth division was created. One infantry battalion was kept as reinforcements in England for every two battalions in France.

If the Deputy Minister of Militia was optimistic, the Prime Minister was exalted. On New Year's Eve, 1915, Sir Robert Borden surprised the nation by announcing that the Canadian army would be doubled and that he intended to place 500,000 men in uniform. It is hard to regard the Prime Minister's action as anything other than an impulse, for he made the dramatic announcement without consulting his advisers or cabinet colleagues and without any study of the over-all Canadian manpower situation, of the effect upon agriculture and industry, or of the dangers to Canadian unity inherent in the plan. To set the actual strength of the Canadian army arbitrarily at half a million men was an act of emotion rather than reason, and in spite of sharp criticism from the well-informed it was on the whole accepted emotionally by the public.

The immediate response to Borden's announcement was encouraging; during the first five months of 1916 a total of 128,273 men enlisted in the Canadian Expeditionary Force, bringing its strength to slightly over 312,000. Thereafter, however, recruiting fell off badly, and it soon became apparent that to achieve an actual army strength of 500,000, the voluntary system of enlistment might have to be abandoned for conscription.

Canadian casualties in Flanders had already been heavy – and this was still before the Battle of the Somme. By the end of 1916, although there had been 384,450 enlistments, the actual strength of the Canadian army was only 299,937. Nearly 100,000 men had been discharged as casualties or for other reasons. A National Service Board was established in October 1916 headed briefly by Sir Thomas Tait and then by R. B. Bennett. It was intended that the board should, in the words of Sir Robert Borden, "make an appeal for voluntary national service which would render unnecessary any resort to compulsion". A voluntary manpower inventory was not a success, and a conference of recruiting officers was told that "the National Service Registration was a farce. No recruits are being obtained from the lists of men being sent to Districts . . . the Registration resulted in thousands of eligible men leaving the Winnipeg District for the States." In December the Chief of the General Staff recommended that compulsion be adopted, but the minister refused to consider it at that time. In the spring of 1917 an attempt to raise a home defence force that would release volunteers for service overseas failed dismally and was abandoned in June.

The war, in fact, was proving a most serious drain on the manpower of all the belligerents. On February 11, 1917, the British Secretary of State for the Colonies, Walter Long, pointed out to the Governor General of Canada that "England, Scotland and Wales have already each furnished over 17 per cent male population to [the] Army to December

[1916]", and suggested that Canada should raise further complete divisions or additional infantry brigades. A formal reply to the British government's suggestion was made on April 3 when copies of an order in council setting forth the Canadian government's views were sent to London. The Canadian government stated that it realized the gravity of the situation and desired to co-operate to the fullest possible extent, but "in view of the large number of men so far recruited for the various Overseas Forces, amounting now to nearly 400,000, and the consequent serious inroads made on the labour supply available to the Dominion", difficulty was being found in providing for the upkeep of the force already in the field. "The Government has had so far to proceed by voluntary enlistment," the order in council went on, "and has now reached the stage when its appeal is addressed to a public whose fit and sympathetic manhood has been very largely abstracted. It does not seem advisable at present to attempt to resort to compulsory methods, which would arouse antagonism and bitterness in various sections of the country . . . under the circumstances, it is considered inadvisable to encourage the hope of our being able to mobilize new divisions or to raise any considerable number of additional fighting units. The Prime Minister of Canada is now in England and the issues involved will no doubt be discussed by him with His Majesty's Government."

Sir Robert Borden, in fact, had been attending meetings of the Imperial War Cabinet in London since March 20. The Imperial War Cabinet, under the chairmanship of Lloyd George, consisted of the five members of the British War Cabinet plus the Dominion prime ministers,* but the conduct of the war was not dealt with by this body. The matter was reserved for the British War Cabinet. By now Sir Robert Borden had become increasingly disillusioned, not indeed with the imperial ideal, but with the methods by which it worked in practice. He protested that "statesmen of the British Isles" did not consult the Dominions as to war policy or even inform them of what was taking place. On January 4, 1916, he had written Sir George Perley, the Canadian High

---

* Australia was not represented at this conference because of the general election then being conducted in that Dominion.

Commissioner in London: "During the past four months . . . the Canadian Government (except for an occasional telegram from you or Sir Max Aitken) have had just what information could be gleaned from the daily press and no more. As to consultation, plans of campaign have been made and unmade, measures adopted and apparently abandoned and generally speaking steps of the most important and even vital character have been taken, postponed or rejected without the slightest consultation with the authorities of this Dominion.

"It can hardly be expected that we shall *put 400,000 or 500,000 men in the field* and willingly accept the position of having no more voice and receiving no more consideration than if we were toy automata."

In 1917 the Dominions were provided with "the confidential and secret reports of the Imperial General Staff and of the Commanders-in-Chief in the various theatres of operations as well as the naval advisers of the Admiralty", but the Dominion prime ministers had no voice in strategy. At the Imperial Conference of 1917 Britain and the Dominions met ostensibly as equals, although Britain was still more equal than the others. Sir Robert Borden recorded that "Britain was *primus inter pares*".

On May 15 he returned to the Canadian House of Commons with a gold mace presented to Canada by the Lord Mayor of London and with the conviction that it would be necessary ". . . to provide, by compulsory military enlistment on a selective basis, such reinforcements as may be necessary to maintain the Canadian Army today in the field as one of the finest fighting units of the Empire. The number of men required will be not less than 50,000 and will probably be 100,000."

Borden's cabinet colleagues had been mistaken in their belief that Sir Robert would have discussed "the issues involved" with His Majesty's Government. At least Borden repudiated this idea in the House of Commons: "Some people afflicted with a diseased imagination have asserted that I took my present course at the request or dictation of the British Government," he said. "No more absolute falsehood was ever uttered by human lips. The subject was never discussed between myself and any member of the British Government; if there had been any such suggestion from them, I, for one, would not have tolerated it."

On May 29 Borden invited the leader of the Liberal opposition, Sir Wilfrid Laurier, to join a coalition government that would pass the military service bill he considered necessary, but after a week's reflection Laurier declined, declaring that conscription should not be introduced unless it was approved by a majority of voters at a new general election. Organized labour opposed compulsory military service; huge anti-conscription meetings were held throughout Quebec, and Archbishop Bruchési of Montreal reminded Sir Robert Borden that he had frequently in the past promised that there would be no conscription and asked what had happened in England or at the front to make him change his mind.

Borden did not introduce the Military Service Bill into Parliament until June 11, by which time the division in Canada was deep and bitter. The ensuing debate in the Canadian Parliament was almost unprecedented in its acrimony. Mr. J. W. Edward, member for Frontenac, accused Laurier of "planting the seeds of distrust and suspicion of Britain in the French-Canadian mind" and of fostering the desire for Canadian independence. "Do not," he said, "wait until the German puts his dirty foot on our Canadian soil and butchers our women and children before taking up arms." Another member declared that the only reason why Canada as a whole was faced with conscription was that French Canada had failed to do her duty.

The Prime Minister was supported by his own Conservative Party and by a large number of conscriptionist Liberals; most French Canadians, whether Liberal, Conservative, or Nationalist, opposed conscription. The Military Service Act made all male British subjects between the ages of twenty and forty-five liable for military service but provided for generous exemptions that were to be granted by special tribunals established in each military district. Borden, remembering that Australia had rejected compulsory military service the previous year by a plebiscite, still hoped that conscription could be introduced without a general election, and on July 17 he asked Parliament to extend its term for a year. He obtained the usual party majority for this resolution, but this was obviously insufficient, and an election was called for December 17.

Before then, between August 31 and September 14, the Conservative majority, after three times invoking closure, passed two extraordinary bills, the War-Times Election Act and the Military Voters' Act, which were designed to ensure the conscriptionists a majority at the polls. The Conservative Party, shaken by scandals and sensing the dissatisfaction in the country, was frankly afraid it would lose the election. "Our ministers," Sir Robert Borden noted in his diary, "afraid of a genl election. Think we wd be beaten."

The answer to this fear was a gigantic gerrymander, designed by Arthur Meighen, the Solicitor General, and defended by him as necessary. By special legislation tampering with the franchise, the vote was given for the duration of the war and the demobilization period to the wives, widows, mothers, sisters, and daughters of any person, male or female, living or dead, who was serving outside Canada in the Canadian or British forces. Concurrently, all conscientious objectors and all naturalized Canadian citizens of enemy birth or extraction who had been naturalized since 1902 were disenfranchised. Soldiers were not allowed to vote for individual candidates, but could vote only for or against the government, and instead of voting for a candidate in his own home riding a soldier could have his vote applied to any electoral district in Canada, a convenient device for strengthening government candidates who were not sure of a normal majority. In defending these pieces of legislation, Arthur Meighen did not endear himself to democrats by speaking of the franchise as a privilege rather than as a right.

Some of these measures were certainly unconstitutional and the disenfranchisement of naturalized Canadian citizens, in theory at least, left any group of Canadian voters at the mercy of a temporary party majority in the House of Commons. Sir Wilfrid Laurier was appalled by the drift of events. In a letter to a friend he wrote: ". . . Ontario is no longer Ontario: it is again the old province of Upper Canada, and again governed from London . . . Upper Canada was governed from Downing Street with the instrumentality of the Family Compact sitting at York, now Toronto. Canada is now governed by a junta sitting at London, known as 'the round table', with ramifications in Toronto, in Winnipeg, in Victoria, with Tories and Grits receiving their ideas from London, and insidiously forcing them on their respective parties." By now, however, Laurier had lost much support, and in September Borden swore in ten former Liberals as cabinet ministers in a new Union government.

A fortnight before the election, alarmed at reports that rural Ontario ridings were likely to vote Liberal, the election headquarters of the Unionist Party held a special conference in Ottawa which resulted in a public pledge from the Minister of Militia, General S. C. Mewburn,* that farmers' sons would not be conscripted. For the first time there began to be serious talk in Quebec of secession from Confederation, and a bill to effect this was actually introduced in the Quebec Legislature.

When Major-General Sir Arthur Currie was promoted to command the Canadian Corps that summer, Sir Robert Borden cabled Sir George Perley: "As soon as Currie is appointed, I shall send message of congratulations to him. It would be well if in his reply he would make clear the need for reinforcements to maintain Canadian Army Corps at full strength. Liberal Press of Quebec are insisting with great vehemence that no further reinforcements are required." Currie replied as had been suggested, but when he was approached again in November he complained about "being bothered by an election" and wrote to Perley: "I do not consider it fair that in the propaganda issued by the Government my name should appear so prominently."

By now the Canadians had been thrown into Passchendaele, and Borden's government, through the Canadian High Commissioner in London, approached Sir Douglas Haig with the request that they be taken out of the line "to recuperate where they could be visited and their votes secured". A strong appeal was made to Canadian soldiers to support the Unionist government, and they were promised that the Military Service Act would be enforced "with vigour and promptitude".

The election, not unexpectedly, gave Borden's new Union-

---

* Sir Sam Hughes had finally been forced to resign in November 1916.

ist government a sweeping majority, 153 seats to 82 – but 62 of the 82 Liberal seats were in Quebec. The popular vote told a different story and reflected far more accurately the real split in the country. The civilian vote in Prince Edward Island, Nova Scotia, Quebec, and the Yukon went against the government, and the total civilian vote for all Canada was 841,944 for the government and 744,849 against it, giving the conscriptionists a civilian majority of only 97,095. The soldiers' vote, however, was 215,849 in favour of the government and 18,522 against. In any case, the country was divided as never before in its history.

In effect, the Military Service Act did more to win the election than to win the war. In Ontario, of the 124,965 men called up in Class I, 116,092 claimed exemption; in Quebec 113,291 claimed exemption out of 115,602. The percentage of claims refused in Quebec was 9.0, while in Ontario it was 8.2. Throughout Canada, of the 401,882 Class I men registered, exemptions were granted to 221,949; defaulters numbered 24,139; and another 26,225 were not called up. Of the 129,569 enlisted, 8,445 went into the British forces and 121,124 into the Canadian Expeditionary Force. Of the 121,124 enlisted in the Canadian army, 21,473 were discharged for medical or other reasons and more than 16,000 were granted harvest or compassionate leave. Thus by the end of the war the Military Service Act had provided a total of 83,355 recruits for the Canadian army. Of this number only 47,509 were sent overseas, and only 24,132 were taken on strength of units serving in France. To obtain these 24,132 men the country had been deeply divided, French had been set against English, Catholic against Protestant, farmer against urbanite, soldier against civilian, and worker against employer.

Passions flared on both sides, and, although the Catholic hierarchy in Quebec steadily counselled moderation and obedience to the law, ugly religious overtones were injected into the controversy. In Ontario, the Grand Master of the Orange Lodge publicly declared that "if the occasion should arise, 250,000 Orangemen, too old for overseas service, could be enlisted in a month to put down the province of Quebec". In Quebec, the nationalist Henri Bourassa called the war "the work of maniacs who glorify a horrible butchery in which people slaughter each other without knowing why". And an anti-imperialist from Quebec angrily said: "We French Canadians owe England nothing but forgiveness."

During Easter week of 1918 serious riots broke out in Quebec City when federal police arrested a French-Canadian civilian named Mercier who had left his exemption papers at home. Mercier was released when his papers were found to be in order, but the disturbances had already begun. The offices of two Conservative newspapers, the *Chronicle* and *L'Evénement*, were sacked; a force of 700 soldiers was sent from Toronto; and on the evening of April 1, Easter Monday, the rioters opened fire on the Ontario troops, wounding four of them. The soldiers replied with rifles and machine guns and cavalry charged the crowd with drawn swords. Four civilians were killed, an undetermined number wounded, and fifty-eight arrested. On April 4 the Borden government suspended *habeas corpus* in Quebec City by order in council, and in the House of Commons Sir Sam Hughes, the former Minister of Militia, asserted that French Canada had been perverted by German propaganda.

Throughout the rest of the country, however, and especially in the rural areas, there was also a growing resistance to conscription. The government broke its promise not to conscript farmers' sons, and the farmers, who had gladly voted for conscription when they thought it would be applied only to other people, were outraged. When more than 5,000 angry farmers from Ontario and the Prairies marched on Ottawa in April, they were told by Prime Minister Borden that he had "a still more solemn covenant" with the troops in France. In Calgary and Toronto there were anti-conscription disturbances, and although these did not receive the publicity given to similar outbreaks in Quebec, they indicated a widespread hostility to the Military Service Act. It was noted that the United States would have to send six million men overseas before it contributed to the war in the same proportion as had Canada and that the shipping shortage meant that for every Canadian reinforcement draft sent across the Atlantic an American draft had to be postponed.

During the latter part of March and the beginning of April 1918, when General Ludendorff's armies were making frightening and unprecedented gains, Prime Minister Lloyd George urgently cabled the Canadian government asking for more men. At a secret session of the House of Commons on April 17 Sir Robert Borden tabled an order in council cancelling all exemptions granted under the Military Service Act and lowering the age limit of conscription from 20 to 19. Laurier challenged the right of the Governor in Council to alter an Act of Parliament. But Borden was undeterred, and when the Supreme Court of Alberta ruled on June 28 that the order in council did not have the force of law, he issued a further order in council which ruled that the previous one should have effect despite adverse judicial decisions by any court.

Canada was now well into the fourth year of the war. Victory seemed as far away as ever — and more necessary. After so much bloodshed, heartache, and disappointment, few British Canadians would have been willing to accept any other outcome of the war.

After Passchendaele the Canadian Corps spent a relatively quiet winter. There was an uneasy calm along most of the Western Front, and it made the Allies apprehensive. In this they had reason on their side, for 1917 had marked the nadir of the Allied cause. With Russia out of the war, the French army convalescing after mutiny, and the British army convalescing after Passchendaele, the outlook for early 1918 was most ominous.

The Germans spent the winter moving troops from the Eastern Front to the Western Front and in training their armies in the new offensive tactics they intended to adopt. Ludendorff had decided that, as soon as spring came, he would stake everything in an attempt to win a decisive victory. Some German senior officers considered his decision too much of a gamble and would have preferred to take up strong defensive positions while at the same time opening negotiations for a compromise peace. It may be doubted that this course of action was politically feasible, but certainly, if the Germans were to succeed, they would have to do so quickly – before summer came, and, with summer, the Americans.

On March 21 Ludendorff's armies surged forward in their third great offensive of the war in the West. The other two had been the initial invasion of France and Belgium in 1914 and Falkenhayn's assault on Verdun. Both these operations had failed, although by narrow margins. Now, however, the Germans had developed an entirely new doctrine for the attack, just as they had done the previous year for the defensive. They decentralized tactical control to the infantry section; they abandoned the concept of linear waves of attackers advancing at a uniform rate and in aligned formation and adopted instead the tactics of infiltration, so that their assault was not a battering ram pounding head-on against a wall but rather a flood of water that flowed along the path of least resistance, isolating obstacles without immediately attempting to overcome them.

Ludendorff's March offensive broke clean through General Gough's Fifth British Army, which virtually ceased to exist as a fighting entity, and captured 500 guns in the first two days. By early April the Germans were threatening the vital rail junction of Amiens. However, General Foch, who was appointed "co-ordinator" of the Allied armies in the threatened sector, sent twenty-one French divisions to bolster Haig's front, the British fought back doggedly, and by April 5 Ludendorff called a halt.

Four days later he struck again, this time in Flanders, and again the Germans made fighting gains, but by April 29 they had just failed to take Ypres, and Ludendorff paused a second time. The third blow hit the French on the Chemin des Dames on May 27; by the time Ludendorff halted the offensive, German troops had reached the Marne and were threatening Paris. The Germans had made far greater advances than any that had been seen on the Western Front since the early weeks of the war, but the new German doctrines of infiltration and the reinforcement of success were better applied at the tactical than at the strategical level. If Ludendorff had gambled everything on his initial March offensive and had reinforced it properly, it might have succeeded and won the war. Instead, the law of diminishing returns began to operate as German casualties mounted. Each succeeding offensive was less intense than its predecessor, and the fourth attack, which was launched on July 15 against the French on the Marne, petered out by August 6.

Ludendorff's last throw had failed, for Marshal Foch, who had been promoted and appointed Allied commander-in-chief, was preparing a counter-thrust. This was to be delivered on August 8 near Amiens, and the Canadians were to play a prominent part in the operation.

General Currie had first let his divisional commanders into the secret on July 29. All had been well satisfied with the news that action was imminent, for they knew their troops had taken the measure of the enemy. General Sir A. C. Macdonell, commander of the 1st Division, for instance, firmly believed that the "Old Red Patch" was the best division in any army anywhere on the globe. And he may have been right, too, although General Sir H. E. Burstall, General L. J. Lipsett, and General Sir David Watson would probably have claimed the same for the 2nd, 3rd, and 4th divisions respectively.

Certainly the Canadians were in fine fighting trim, for they had been well rested during the spring and summer. None of Ludendorff's attacks had fallen on portions of the front which they had been holding. In May and June they had not been in the line at all, and in July they had held only quiet sectors. Reinforcement drafts had filled the ranks depleted at Passchendaele; an intensive program of sports and training had left the men fit, brown, and hard; and, most important, morale was as high as it had ever been. The stupidities and horrors of Passchendaele were things of the past, and every soldier seemed to have a sixth sense that the tide of war had turned at last.

This feeling was not brought about entirely by the final failure of Ludendorff's offensive, or by the quarter of a million fresh American troops who were now arriving in France each month, or even by the heartening fact that, after four divisive years, the Allied armies were finally unified under Marshal Foch. Perhaps it was a compound of all this; perhaps it was something less tangible; but at all events, for the first time in the long, long war, the fighting troops themselves – and not just the high command – scented victory in the air.

Even the tactics of the Battle of Amiens were different and more promising. Currie had emphasized to his divisional commanders that for once the high command was insisting that complete secrecy be observed. Not even brigadiers and battalion commanders would be told of the attack ahead of time. The Canadian Corps would move south from the Orange

Hill area to Amiens entirely by night; units would remain under cover by day; forward reconnaissance would be strictly limited; wireless silence would be imposed; Allied air forces would dominate the sky above the concentration area to prevent any German observation plane from discovering what was going on; and every soldier would have a notice pasted in the back of his pay book, warning him in big letters to "Keep Your Mouth Shut". Important too was the fact that this time the Allied attack was to go in against a relatively weak sector of the German front. General von der Marwitz's Second Army consisted of fourteen divisions, but only two of them were fully fit for battle and all were well below establishment. The German field defences were not strong and there were none of the concrete pillboxes and deep belts of barbed wire that had made other German positions so formidable.

Two Canadian battalions were to be sent into the line near Mount Kemmel in Flanders so that the enemy could identify them there, two Canadian casualty clearing stations would open in the same area, and a Canadian wireless unit would busily send out fake messages in a code the Germans could read. The enemy must get no inkling that the Canadian Corps was concentrating near Amiens, for since the Canadians were recognized as élite troops their presence would be a sure sign an attack was imminent. This time, too, no preliminary bombardment would give warning of what was in store, and the 604 Allied tanks allotted to the assault would form up at night, the noise of their approach being drowned by the roar of bomber planes flying up and down the front line.

The plan called for General Eugène Debeney's First French Army and General Sir H. S. Rawlinson's Fourth British Army to attack between the Avre and Ancre rivers with twenty-one divisions, supported by 3,676 guns. The Canadian Corps would attack in the centre, flanked by the 31st and 9th French corps on the right and by the Australian Corps and 3rd British Corps on the left. In the Canadian sector the 1st Division would be in the centre, with the 3rd Division on the right and the 2nd on the left; the 4th Division would be in reserve. Each of the three assaulting divisions was given forty-two fighting tanks which were to advance with the infantry and deal with machine guns and barbed wire. Each division also had six supply tanks which were to maintain the momentum of the advance by delivering ammunition, water, and engineer stores to the infantry.

The Canadian battle was planned in three phases. The initial objective, the Green Line, was some two miles inside the German front; the intermediate objective, or Red Line, was on the average about a mile and a half farther on. In the final phase the Cavalry Corps and the 4th Division were to pass through the Red Line to the final objectives of the day on the Dotted Blue Line east of the villages of Caix and Le Quesnel which were between seven and eight miles distant from the original front. A mixed force of machine guns and 6-inch mortars under Brigadier-General R. Brutinel would provide right flank protection.

The Canadians began to move to their concentration area at the end of July. In their railway boxcars the men played poker, Seven-toed Pete, and Black Jack while they speculated as to their destination. The hopeful ones declared they were being transferred to the Italian front; the more pessimistic were certain they were returning to the Ypres Salient. Part of the journey was made in fleets of buses that raced wildly through the night, hurrying like so many vampires to get out of sight before dawn. The last stretch was covered by the infantry on foot.

On the last few nights before the attack, as soon as darkness fell, the roads about Amiens were jammed with troops, guns, tanks, motor vehicles, and supply wagons, all moving east. Only the occasional staff car or dispatch rider on a motorcycle squeezed by in the opposite direction. The Canadians swung along cheerily, and for the first time since the Somme the men sang on the march. Their songs were less sentimental than those of 1914, but no one complained about that. One immortal favourite went:

> When this bloody war is over,
> Oh how happy I will be!
> No more pork and beans for breakfast,
> No more bully beef for tea.
> When I get my civvy clothes on,
> No more soldiering for me . . .

Canadian Scottish units found their pipe bands halted and waiting for them 4,000 yards in rear of the assembly areas. Since the skirl of the bagpipes carries long distances, the bands remained where they were for the time being, but the Highlanders marched forward with the music of "Scotland the Brave" ringing in their ears, and with the knowledge that on the day of the attack their pipers, as always, would be with the assault waves.

Under dark, moonless skies the marching columns tramped down the steep hill to the hamlet of Boves, crossed the Avre stream, and went up the long steady slope to Gentelles Wood, which was soon crammed to overflowing with camouflaged gun pits, ammunition dumps, engineer stores, tanks in laager, and bivouacking troops. Here no fires were allowed by night and military police kept watch to see that no smoke rose above the treetops by day. If the enemy discovered the Canadian concentration, his artillery would have magnificent targets, but the security precautions were effective. The last Canadian units were in place by 2 A.M. on August 8, and the night remained quiet except for a steady roll of distant gunfire to the north near Villers-Bretonneux.

At zero hour, which was at 4.20 A.M., the Canadian infantry went forward more dispersed than usual and with lighter loads. Nevertheless, each man still carried 250 rounds of ammunition, his gas mask, his water bottle, iron rations of bully beef and biscuit, an entrenching tool, two Mills bombs, and two sandbags. This advance, however, was not merely the customary slogging ahead at the high port behind the barrage. There was more dash to it, more confidence, and more enthusiasm.

The fog helped. When the Canadian barrage suddenly roared out like some vicious beast, the ground mist was so dense that a man could not see farther than twenty yards. In the valley of the Luce nothing could be distinguished more than five yards away. Each platoon of the nine assaulting battalions had to grope its way forward independently, guided by its own officer on a compass bearing.

No-man's-land, untouched by any preliminary bombardment, was crossed easily and the sparse German wire gave little trouble. The earth about the enemy front line was pock-

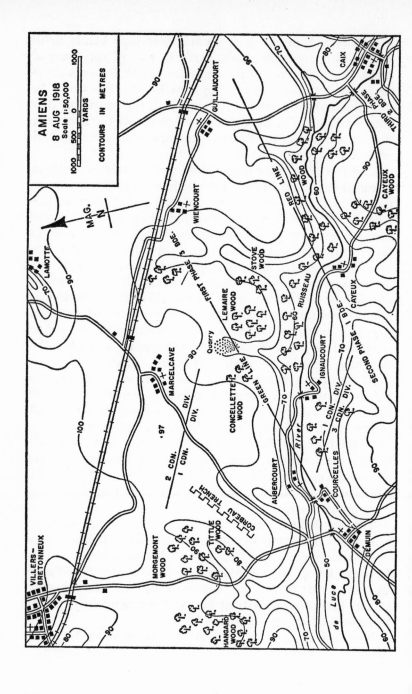

Field Marshal Sir Douglas Haig (right) with General Sir Arthur
Currie, February 1918

The 28th Battalion marching past Sir Robert Borden, July 1918

Canadian troops filling their water bottles near Amiens, August 1918

Canadians resting in captured trenches during the advance east
of Arras, August 1918

A Canadian patrol crosses the square at Cambrai, October 1918.
The retreating Germans left many parts of the city ablaze.

These photographs taken in April and May 1919 show the devastation left by the war: UPPER LEFT the village of Festubert; LOWER LEFT Duck's Bill Crater, scene of bitter fighting near Givenchy, June 1915; ABOVE one of the craters at St. Eloi where Canadian troops were engaged in heavy fighting in April 1916.

The ruins of the village of Givenchy in the spring of 1919

marked with fresh shell holes, still smoking with nitrate fumes and with fine grains of moist brown earth around their rims. The defenders had no chance. The terrible drum-fire of the barrage no sooner lifted than the Canadians were upon them, looming up suddenly out of the mist. Dead Germans littered the trenches and many prisoners were rounded up before they could make a stand. Yet there were no signs of poor enemy morale. Only a few weeks previously the German armies had gored deep holes in the Allied lines, and most prisoners were unwilling to admit that all hope of victory had gone. When asked who was going to win the war, they would only shrug their shoulders and say they did not know.

During the advance to the Green Line the 1st and 2nd divisions both attacked with one brigade up, while the 3rd Division on the right, expecting more difficult going, advanced on a two-brigade front. On the left the 2nd Division took the village of Marcelcave, and fresh troops then passed through to capture the hamlets of Wiencourt and Guillaucourt. In the centre the 1st Division cleared Hangard Wood and Morgemont Wood, captured the village of Aubercourt, and was on the Green Line by 8.15 A.M. In spite of a shortage of Mills bombs, one Canadian battalion captured nineteen guns, seven mortars, and thirty-one machine guns before noon. Several other Canadian units did as well. On the right the 3rd Division took Cemetery Copse and the village of Hangard, captured the hamlet of Demuin and Hamon Wood, and pressed on past the Green Line to overrun Rifle Wood. The battalions in this sector had to perform some fairly intricate manoeuvres in open country, but they took out the opposing machine-gun nests with rifle grenades, bombs, and Lewis guns just as they had practised doing during their summer's training.

On either side of the tree-lined River Luce which flowed parallel to the Canadian axis of advance through the centre of the corps sector, unfenced fields of wheat, oats, and rye stood ready for the reaper. The grain fields gave excellent cover for German machine-gunners, many of whom were left to be dealt with by the supporting waves. Some tanks, blinded by the mist, fell behind, and some stuck in the soft ground of the Luce valley, but those that kept pace were invaluable in winkling out the numerous German machine guns that were deployed in great depth across the front. At a sunken road in the 3rd Division's sector a few Whippets took a line of enemy machine-gun nests in enfilade with their Hotchkiss guns and within seconds turned the lane into a bloody shambles. An infantryman rode in each tank and co-operation was better than ever before, thanks to the summer's intensive training.

The supporting battalions, coming forward a little later and clearing out pockets of bypassed enemy resistance as they advanced, could scarcely believe that the attack was going so well. As they pressed deeper into enemy country, German prisoners filed back past them to the rear, first in little groups, then in a growing stream: Saxons, Bavarians, Westphalians – some still sleepy, some shaken by the sudden intensity of the attack, some sullen and indignant at finding the Canadians on their front when their intelligence had assured them that those dreaded shock troops were miles away in the Ypres Salient in Flanders. Many prisoners had the battalion numbers of their captors chalked on their backs.

A mile or so beyond the ruptured German front a group of Canadian officers clustered around a disabled tank and listened eagerly while a wounded British sergeant, lying on a stretcher and waiting for an ambulance to take him to a dressing station, told how the morning had gone: "Tanks slap through 'is artillery," the sergeant said between puffs on a cigarette. "Canadians out in the open! Blimey, we done it on 'im this time!"

At the crossings of the River Luce the engineers strung waist-high telephone wire to guide the troops through the mist. The duckboards over the stream had to be traversed in single file, but traffic control was good and little delay resulted. Although German 5.9's intermittently shelled the valley, they caused few casualties. The heavy artillery gave useful support in the second phase of the attack, but the field guns had not sufficient range to provide a barrage between the Green and Red lines. However, this was not too serious, since enemy resistance was much weaker now.

Once the machine guns had been overcome, the attack

picked up momentum, although now that it was full daylight many tanks were hit by German guns firing over open sights. As the enemy fell back in increasing disorder, little groups of grey-clad soldiers streaming eastward suffered heavy casualties from Canadian Lewis-gun and rifle fire.

The German gun areas were quickly overrun. Some guns were captured before they got into action, their sleepy-looking crews being rounded up while they were still pulling off the tarpaulins. Some batteries, on the other hand, fought gallantly over open sights until the gunners were bombed or bayoneted. One company of the 42nd Battalion (Royal Highlanders of Canada) in a series of rushes got to within 150 yards of three 8-inch howitzers and an anti-tank gun that were firing at them at point-blank range. Then the Highlanders charged with fixed bayonets and killed or captured the gun crews. A few minutes later another 42nd company captured a battery of 4.1-inch howitzers after sweeping them with Lewis-gun fire. By the time the reserve waves reached the German gun area, many captured pieces were already in action, manned by specially trained Canadian crews.

As the climbing sun dispelled the mist, a beautiful summer day was revealed, warm but with a light wind. From the Canadian centre much of the battlefield was visible through binoculars. A battered line of telegraph poles along the railway line running between Villers-Bretonneux and Chaulnes marked the corps's northern boundary; south of the railway the church steeple at Wiencourt and the Norman tower of the church at Guillaucourt poked up above the treetops, while down in the 3rd Division's sector the Le Quesnel church spire was wreathed with black shell-bursts. Beyond the line of tall elms lining the Amiens-Roye road, which was the Canadian southern boundary, tiny figures in French horizon-blue could be seen assembling to attack Moreuil Wood. Their long bayonets glinted in the sunlight, while the French 75's, firing with the peculiar rapidity which was their hallmark and their pride, sent a moving storm of shrapnel driving across the wood.

On the 2nd Division's front the Red Line was reached by 2.15 P.M. In the centre the assaulting battalions were all on the Red Line between 11.00 and 11.30 A.M., while in the 3rd

Division's sector the intermediate objectives were all taken between 10.00 and 10.20 A.M.

Canadian batteries were leapfrogged forward to support the advance, but late in the morning there came a time when the enemy artillery had been overrun and the Canadian guns were either out of range or without targets. A strange hush fell over the battlefield. Soldiers sat down in the open fields to eat a picnic lunch of bully beef and biscuit, supplemented by cabbage, onions, and carrots from near-by farms. The warm August day in rural Picardy was as still and peaceful as a Sunday at home. The open, rolling countryside east of Amiens was broken only by sleepy little villages surrounded by walled orchards and deep, cool woods. Fields of ripening grain rippled in a playful breeze and the waters of the River Luce gurgled happily beneath overhanging willows at the bottom of the valley.

At first the soldiers lying on the grass by the river bank could not identify the new sound. It was still a long way off and very faint, and – perhaps because it was not immediately menacing – it did not thrust itself to the forefront of their consciousness. They ignored it for a time or listened idly, their minds elsewhere.

The background noise was nearer now, and a few infantrymen raised their heads to stare at each other incredulously. The sound was unmistakable. It was the drumming of thousands of horses' hooves. The soldiers jumped to their feet and looked back the way they had come. There, down the Valley Road between the hamlets of Domart and Hangard, regiment after regiment of cavalry were advancing in fours at a steady trot. A cloud of white dust, drifting sideways from the road, marked the progress of the column, and in the open fields on either side light Whippet tanks clanked briskly along like sheep dogs patrolling a flock. Sun flashes winked like a hundred heliographs from lances and drawn sabres as the cavalry drew nearer. The horsemen trotted up to the crossings of the Luce, put their mounts down the steep bank, and splashed through the water with a pretty flurry of jingling harness and flying spray. They breasted the rise on the far side of the stream, swung out into extended line in the fields beyond, touched spurs to their horses, and galloped off towards the horizon. It was a sight not to be seen again in war.

Thus the cavalry at last went through – for the first time in four years of a war in which millions of men had lived like moles underground, had measured their advances and retirements in yards, and had paid for both with casualties by the thousand. Time and again the Allied generals had dreamed of this day, and time and again they had been disappointed. New trench lines as strong as the old had formed like scabs over each slight break in the enemy line. Only on this single occasion had the Allies achieved a real breakthrough on the Western Front.

The cavalry passed on and fresh infantry battalions pushed forward to exploit the victory, but the illusion of peace persisted. Only in the sky, where a number of dogfights had broken out, was there tangible evidence of war. Many soldiers watched the low-level aerial combats through captured German field glasses. An unprecedented amount of booty had been taken that morning. Officers found it necessary to confiscate quite a few demijohns of cognac – "Fritzie rum" – that were passing too freely among the troops; harsh German cigarettes were plentiful for anyone who wanted them, as were the rank but smokable German cigars; quantities of rock candy, rain capes, and Luger automatics had been captured; and some lucky soldiers had even obtained one of the increasingly rare, spiked leather helmets, or *Pickelhauben*, that were so much prized as souvenirs.

In the final phase, the 2nd Division on the right reached the Dotted Blue Line by early evening. In the centre, the 1st Division, assisted by the cavalry, was on its last objective by 2.30 P.M., and on the left the 4th Division passed through the 3rd Division at 12.40 P.M., about two hours after the cavalry had gone through.

In general, the cavalry actions on August 8 were notably less successful than those of the infantry. This was due to no lack of *élan*, but merely to the obvious fact that a horseman presented a better target than a man on foot. Both Lord Strathcona's Horse and the Royal Canadian Dragoons were heavily engaged in the afternoon, but the 4th Division's infantry battalions came up with the cavalry within a mile of the Red Line in the vicinity of Beaucourt Wood. The wood was cleared by 4.30 P.M., but the village of Le Quesnel was not taken before dark.

During the afternoon, captive balloons were hauled forward to float like huge sausages over the newly won ground. That evening the Canadians ate hot dinners from their own company cookers and many soldiers bedded down comfortably on stooks of harvested grain. As darkness fell, the enemy could be heard blowing up ammunition dumps to the east, and German planes came over to drop random bombs.

In a single day's fighting the Canadian Corps had driven forward eight miles to help win what was far and away the greatest Allied victory of the war on the Western Front. All Canadian objectives were taken, except for a small pocket of resistance at Le Quesnel which was cleared up before dawn the next day. The other Allied attacks had done nearly as well. The Australians had advanced seven miles, the French five, and the British two. The Canadians had liberated ten villages, taken 5,033 prisoners – considerably more than their total casualties – and captured 161 guns. Canadian losses for the day were 3,868, of which 1,036 were fatal; the Germans lost 650 to 700 officers and 26,000 to 27,000 men.

When the battle was resumed on August 9, surprise, of course, was no longer possible. During the night the enemy had rushed up seven extra divisions and had re-established his line. Even so, the advance would certainly have been more successful had not confusion and countermanded orders at Fourth Army headquarters resulted in a delay of more than five hours.

During the morning in the Canadian sector brigade staffs rode about the open fields with pennants flying, and battalion commanders galloped off to conferences as though on manoeuvres at some peacetime summer camp, but repeated postponements delayed the attack until one o'clock in the afternoon. The 3rd Division was unable to advance until two o'clock. Nevertheless, although the enemy made good use of the time so gratuitously offered him, the Canadians drove forward a maximum of four miles on August 9 and captured the villages of Méharicourt, Rouvroy, and Bouchoir. Casualties for the day amounted to 2,574 men.

On August 10 the Canadians advanced another mile

against continuously stiffening opposition. General Currie recommended that the offensive be halted to give time for the preparation of a set-piece attack. Better yet, he suggested, the Canadian Corps could be withdrawn and employed as shock troops elsewhere. Later in the day, when General Rawlinson visited Field Marshal Haig at Villers-Bretonneux, he brought with him a copy of Currie's recommendations and aerial photographs of the strong German positions. As a result, the battle was ended on August 11. For the next three days the 3rd Division was engaged in some unpleasant fighting as it cleared enemy trenches between Fouquescourt and Parvillers, and the 1st and 4th divisions were committed to local attacks between August 16 and August 20, but on the 20th the Canadians began moving north to the Arras sector.

Since the first attack on August 8, the Canadian Corps had driven forward fourteen miles, had captured more than 9,000 prisoners, and had inflicted heavy casualties on the enemy. Canadian losses had not been light – between the 8th and the 20th they had totalled 11,822 – but for the first time all ranks experienced a quickening hope that the war might really be ended before another winter.

Looking back on it now, we can see that the fighting on the Western Front in 1918 had a distinctive character of its own, different from that of 1915, 1916, and 1917, but different also from that of the summer of 1914. If we were to compare the war to a game of chess (a comparison often made but one of very limited relevance) we might say that the initial campaign of 1914 was an open game, that the fighting in the next three years was a close game, and that the operations of 1918 were a half-open game. In 1918 both German and Allied offensives gained more ground more rapidly than had been possible in the preceding three years, but the breakthroughs were still not sufficiently complete to restore the war of movement that had characterized the opening campaign of the war. The Germans initiated the more open style of warfare with Ludendorff's offensives beginning on March 21, and it was these offensives that determined the course of all the subsequent fighting.

The new German offensive doctrine seemed revolutionary, but it was not so. What the Germans had done was study, understand, and regularize what actually happened on most battlefields in any case. Even at Vimy, probably the most successful example of the set-piece attack, the rate of advance and the success gained had not been uniform across the front. Ludendorff's young men who developed the new offensive tactics considered the attack as having depth as well as frontage and changed their methods of command and support accordingly. Thus they were able to reintroduce flexibility in the attack without losing control of the battle. They did this by looking steadily at reality and adjusting their theoretical concepts to conform to it. The Allied doctrine of the attack, on the other hand, had basically been an attempt to impose a theory upon the realities of the battlefield. The Allied system looked neater on maps, but the German system was the raising to the level of doctrine what every Canadian infantry company had for years actually been doing on the ground whenever it found itself checked by a machine-gun post or a strong-point.

The great German offensives failed (because of strategical and operational rather than tactical errors), but they had opened up the nature of the fighting. At their conclusion the German army was dangerously weak – in itself a factor that favoured deeper Allied penetration and more distant objectives – and the Germans were left holding much recently captured ground that had not yet been prepared for the defence. At Amiens, for instance, the German defences were weak both because of a shortage of manpower and because the German Second Army, standing on newly captured ground, was reluctant to build elaborate defences which it would have to abandon if its advance were resumed.

The Allied gains at Amiens, particularly in the Canadian and Australian sectors, were comparable to the great German gains of the spring – and for the same reasons. The rusty staff work at Fourth Army headquarters seriously affected the battle on the second day, for time is by far the most precious asset that can be given to the defence. Thereafter the Germans reinforced by rail more rapidly than the Allies could feed the advance across country. The momentum of the attack waned, and Currie was brilliantly right to recognize this and recommend a shift of locality. This problem of maintaining the momentum of an attack was never entirely solved in the First World War, for the technological difficulties were too great. The key to its solution, of course, was the internal combustion engine which made possible the mechanization of transport and support services. The introduction to the assault itself of a proper armoured spearhead, capable of sustained cross-country movement and fighting, occasionally produced dramatic results in the Second World War, but by and large the three-ton lorry probably did as much to keep the attack moving as did the tank.

The victory of Amiens had effects much more far-reaching than a mere tactical success. General Erich Ludendorff, now virtually in sole charge of the German war effort, wrote that August 8 was "the black day of the German Army in the history of this war". On August 10 he reported so gloomily to the Kaiser that the German monarch interrupted him to say: "We have reached the limits of our capacity. The war must be ended." A few days later the German government opened peace negotiations through the King of Spain and the Queen of the Netherlands.

The 31st (Alberta) Battalion had been in the line at Arras only seven hours on August 23, 1918, when its first fighting patrols began to slip unobtrusively out of their trenches and work their way forward towards the German positions. This was not a full-scale attack, but only a minor probing operation to locate the enemy, test his alertness, and perhaps wrest some slight tactical advantage from him. By now this type of aggressive domination of no-man's-land was second nature to all Canadian battalions.

Moving from cover to cover, the Alberta men flitted like shadows across the bright August landscape. One patrol reached a sunken road before it was forced to ground by machine-gun fire, and another patrol pushed on and occupied an orchard. These advances sufficiently improved the battalion's position to make possible a surprise attack that night which captured an enemy trench, and, when the unit's scouts reported that a sugar factory south of Neuville-Vitasse could be taken, the battalion promptly went on and occupied the ruined building.

The real significance of this minor action was that early on the morning of August 24 the Germans pulled out of Neuville-Vitasse. Even a month earlier such a prompt withdrawal would have been unlikely, but the commander of the German 39th Infantry Division decided to retire because "the commitment of the Canadians, the best British troops, had been recognized". With Currie's men moving up against them, the Germans were not anxious to defend isolated outposts. The occupation of the sugar factory also helped secure the start line for the next major Canadian offensive. Less than two weeks previously the Canadian Corps had left the Amiens sector as secretly as it had assembled there. The infantry battalions had marched out along white roads under a full moon to be transported by trains and London buses to Arras, where the 2nd and 3rd divisions took over the front from Neuville-Vitasse to the Scarpe River.

After the German defeat at Amiens General Ludendorff had rejected the advice of his defensive expert, von Lossberg, to withdraw at once to the Hindenburg Line. Ludendorff felt that any show of weakness might prejudice Germany's chance of obtaining a "soft peace", and although he himself did not regard the retention of ground as important for its own sake, he had reason to believe that Allied commanders did. The German armies were ordered to defend themselves in their existing positions.

Marshal Foch, however, was determined to give the enemy no respite. In order to prevent German reserves from being concentrated effectively, Foch declined to concentrate all his efforts on a single great offensive, but began instead to strike a series of blows at widely spaced sectors of the front, in the Argonne, in Flanders, on the Somme, and about Arras. On August 20 General Mangin's French Tenth Army of twelve divisions attacked between Compiègne and Soissons, and in two days it drove forward five miles. On the 21st General Humbert's French Third Army attacked on Mangin's left and General Byng's British Third Army struck north of Albert, advancing towards Bapaume and capturing many prisoners. The British Fourth Army assaulted astride the Somme. By August 26 it was the turn of the British First Army, which included the Canadian Corps.

The defences facing the Canadians were at least as strong as any on the entire Western Front. Directly ahead of them the town of Monchy-le-Preux stood on high ground, guarded by advanced positions on Orange Hill and Chapel Hill. Behind Monchy was the Fresnes-Rouvroy Line, and behind this again, and linked to it by the Vis-en-Artois switch, lay the immensely strong Drocourt-Quéant Line, consisting of well-dug front and support trenches, protected by great belts of new barbed wire that glinted with an ominous blue sheen in the August sunlight. Some four miles east of the Drocourt-Quéant Line in front of the city of Cambrai were the Canal du Nord and the formidable defences of the main Hindenburg line which here consisted of two separate trench systems, the Marquion and the Marcoing. The enemy high command considered its positions before Cambrai vital, for if they were pierced the German army would have to fall back on a wide front and fight on ground that had not been prepared for defence. Moreover, if the Allied attacks could not be checked here where the defences were strongest, there was little hope of withstanding assaults elsewhere. Thus the Canadian drive towards Cambrai could not hope to achieve surprise. This was a serious handicap, especially since anything except a straightforward frontal attack was impossible. Time and again in this war Allied armies attempting what the Canadians were now about to undertake had been halted with bloody losses.

However, the four Canadian divisions were by now composed very largely of veterans who had a long record of unbroken success to their credit. Canadian commanders and staffs had also learned much since 1915 and 1916. Infantry, artillery, tanks, and aircraft all knew how to co-operate on the battlefield, to work together as a single co-ordinated machine. Morale was as high as ever and confidence much higher, for after Amiens the Canadians realized that the enemy was near to breaking. In the last hundred days of the war, whenever the Canadian Corps was committed to action, all ranks displayed an inflexible determination to press on to victory. As officers were killed or wounded others took their places so smoothly that the power of the attack was often not checked, even momentarily. Frequently, when no officers were left, platoons and companies would be admirably led by N.C.O.s or even by private soldiers.

General Currie announced his plan to his divisional commanders on August 22. The 2nd and 3rd divisions would assault astride the Arras-Cambrai road, break through the Drocourt-Quéant Line south of the Scarpe River, and advance to the Canal du Nord. The 51st (Highland) Division would be attached to the Canadian Corps for operations north of the Scarpe until the 1st and 4th Canadian divisions arrived on August 25 and August 28, respectively.

The night before the battle was filled with the suppressed tension that always precedes an attack. Men spoke in low voices and gave orders in whispers. By contrast, the sounds that could not be muted – the jingle of harness, the rumble of wheels, the steady tramp of marching columns – seemed louder than usual. It was still dark at three o'clock in the morning of the 26th when the Canadians moved off behind a tremendous artillery barrage. In the initial stages of the attack the guns did much of the work and the infantrymen found the front trenches choked with German dead.

On the right, where Major-General Burstall's 2nd Division was attacking, Chapel Hill was overrun by six o'clock and an hour and a half later the Canadians reached the outskirts of the village of Guémappe. Farther south two battalions attacking towards Wancourt Tower crossed the dry bed of the Cojeul River and drove forward to clear Egret Trench.

On the left Major-General Lipsett's 3rd Division did equally well. Orange Hill fell and the town of Monchy was captured by 7.40. Fresh troops then passed through to clear the woods to the east and capture German trenches south of Monchy. North of the Scarpe River the 51st (Highland) Division kept abreast of the advancing Canadians. As twilight fell that evening a series of German counterattacks, launched from the Bois du Vert and Jigsaw Wood, were smashed by the Canadian guns.

The first day had gone well. For August 27, General Currie ordered the 2nd and 3rd divisions to break through the Fresnes-Rouvroy Line. That night it rained heavily, making the ground slippery and causing the soldiers much discomfort. Company kitchens moved up in the darkness to feed the front-line troops – it was really remarkable how delicious a hot bacon sandwich and a mug of rum-laced coffee tasted at four o'clock in the morning – and at 4.55 the Canadian infantry sprang forward again. One battalion smartly cleared the Bois du Vert, a small, irregular-shaped wood east of Monchy, and another took the Bois du Sart. However, further advances were finally halted by machine-gun fire from Artillery Wood and Jigsaw Wood to the north. In the 3rd Division's sector the villages of Vis-en-Artois and Chérisy were taken and after bitter hand-to-hand fighting with bayonet and bomb the Canadians forced a crossing over the Sensée River late in the afternoon. By now the assault was well into the German gun areas where many artillerymen fought their field guns over open sights until mowed down by Lewis-gun fire.

That night it rained again, but the 28th dawned warm and bright. Casualties and continuous, exhausting fighting were beginning to take their toll, but at first light the Canadian infantry once more stormed ahead.

All three brigades of Major-General Lipsett's 3rd Division attacked in turn, each being supported by the full weight of available artillery. At eleven o'clock the 9th Brigade broke through the Fresnes-Rouvroy Line, then two battalions swung north to clear the village of Boiry–Notre-Dame and Artillery Hill. This done, the artillery switched its fire to the 8th Brigade's front where the infantry took Seventy Ridge, Rémy Wood, Jigsaw Wood, and the village of Pelves. South of the Arras-Cambrai road the assault was equally gallant but less successful. The Canadians broke into the German positions but were driven out again by strong counterattacks late in the evening.

In three days of the most vicious fighting the 2nd and 3rd divisions had advanced more than five miles on an ever-widening front and had captured some 3,300 prisoners, 53 guns, and 519 machine guns. The losses, however, had been tragically severe. No fewer than 254 Canadian officers and 5,547 other ranks had been killed or wounded. Most battalions could muster a trench strength of no more than 200 men, and now, when a unit held an orders group, all its officers could often sit around a single shell hole. Some brigades were down to less than a thousand men.

Yet the enemy was in far worse shape, and the rate of the advance in this type of close country offered strong confirmation that the German army was no longer the fine fighting machine it had once been. By now the German high command was throwing in reserves recklessly, hoping against hope that the inexorable Canadian assaults could be halted, even temporarily, so that with the coming of winter there would be a pause which might make possible a negotiated peace. Fortunately, the weather remained fair and warm during the days, although the sultry nights were oppressive and often rainy. Invariably, as darkness fell, Gotha bombers flew over, the drone of their engines rising and falling in a familiar, unwelcome cadence. Their bombs almost always caused some casualties in Canadian rear areas and their presence made sleeping difficult.

On the night of August 28–29 the 1st Division relieved the 2nd Division and the 4th British Division took over from the 3rd Division. At first light the next morning the relentless assault began again. General Currie, worried about the failure of the 51st (Highland) Division to keep pace north of the Scarpe, formed a composite brigade group under Brigadier-General R. Brutinel for left flank protection. On the 24th Brutinel's brigade captured Bench Farm and Victoria Copse north of Boiry, and the 4th British Division took the villages of Rémy and Haucourt.

On the night of August 30, two battalions of the 1st Brigade marched south into the village of Hendecourt in the 17th Corps's sector. Hendecourt, which had been captured by a gallant British attack the previous day, lay behind the Fresnes-Rouvroy Line, and the 1st Brigade took advantage of this fact to by-pass the strongest portion of the German defences. At 4.40 in the morning two Canadian battalions attacked due north, while another battalion, a mile south of the village of Vis-en-Artois, drove due south. By seven o'clock these converging attacks had linked up near Upton Wood, which was cleared later in the day. The Fresnes-Rouvroy Line was now firmly in Canadian hands. A year ago a success such as this might easily have taken weeks of preparation, followed by a week or more of the bloodiest fighting.

On the 31st the Canadians worked their way forward at dawn and in the face of stiff opposition cleared Ocean Work, an enemy strong-point south of Haucourt. During the night the 4th Division moved into the line between the 1st Division and the 4th British Division. The next day the Canadian infantry captured the Crow's Nest, a heavily defended position on a high bluff overlooking the Drocourt-Quéant Line. The Crow's Nest was held despite desperate German efforts to recapture it.

By now the Canadians had closed with the main German defences west of the Canal du Nord. The fighting, if unspectacular, had been bitter, and much of it had been at close quarters. Gains had been achieved which, had they been made at the Somme or at Passchendaele, would have been hailed throughout the Allied world as a brilliant victory. Now, however, there was no time for self-congratulation. The Drocourt-Quéant position, well-wired, admirably sited, and heavily manned, still lay ahead.

Currie had planned to attack the Drocourt-Quéant Line with three divisions. On the right the 1st Division was to assault with two brigades up, the 4th Division would attack in the centre with one brigade, and the 4th British Division would advance on the left. However, late on the afternoon of August 31 the commander of the 4th British Division informed Currie that his troops were too exhausted to cover the frontage of attack allotted them. As a result, the plan had to be altered at the last minute and the 4th Canadian Division was required to take over half the frontage that was to have been covered by the British. The 10th Brigade had to march ten miles in the darkness, relieve a British brigade, assemble for the attack, and assault at dawn on September 2.

The artillery support the Canadians received was magnificent. The Drocourt-Quéant Line was subjected to a barrage of terrible intensity which pulverized the enemy's front ·and support trenches. As soon as their initial tasks had been fired, selected batteries limbered up and began to leapfrog forward to provide supporting fire for the later stages of the attack.

The 3rd Brigade fought its way through the Drocourt-Quéant defences, captured the village of Cagnicourt, cleared the Bois de Loison, and reached its final objective on the Buissy Switch. It is a measure of the severity of the fighting that seven Canadians were awarded the Victoria Cross on September 2. In the village of Cagnicourt the 14th Battalion (Royal Montreal Regiment) captured a German medical officer in charge of a large dressing station. The doctor, badly

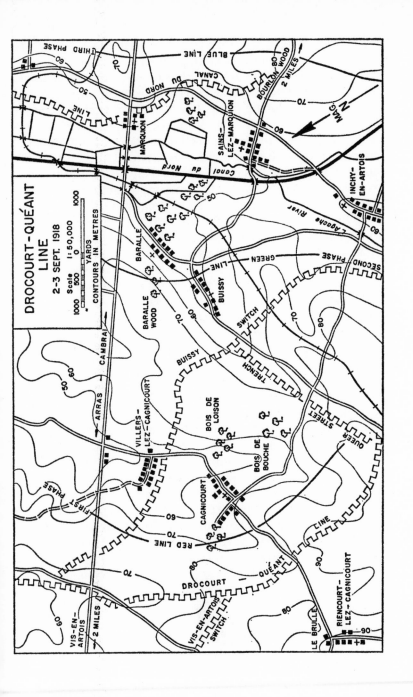

DROCOURT-QUÉANT
LINE
2-3 SEPT. 1918

Scale 1:50,000
1000   500   0   1000
YARDS
CONTOURS IN METRES

frightened, begged the Montreal men in perfect English to spare his life. When he was assured that the Canadians did not kill medical personnel and that both he and his patients were perfectly safe, he picked up his courage and ran forward to intercept a bombing party that was about to clear a cellar. "Wait! I'll get them out," he promised, and with that he hurried through the village from cellar to cellar, calling down to his compatriots below ground. The Germans began to come up by the score, hands raised above their heads and relieved expressions on their faces. As they continued to emerge from their shelters, the prisoners soon greatly outnumbered the 14th Battalion men in Cagnicourt. Before long some 800 Germans had been assembled and sent back to the rear.

To the north, the 4th Division, aided by tanks, cleared its portion of the Drocourt-Quéant Line and advanced to a sunken road running from Drury to the Arras-Cambrai highway. With its last defences west of the Canal du Nord overrun, the German high command came to a hard decision. On the night of September 2–3 the enemy withdrew into the main Hindenburg Line on a broad front extending all the way from the Scarpe to the Aisne. No German units remained facing the Canadians west of the Canal du Nord.

Yet, even so, the advance on September 3 was not without loss. Across the canal, where the towering massif of Bourlon Wood overlooked the countryside for miles around, guns on the forward slope poured a steady fire into the Canadian battalions moving across country. The muzzle-flashes of the German artillery could plainly be seen among the huge oak trees of Bourlon Wood, but the troublesome enemy machine guns, firing at long range from across the canal, were more difficult to locate. To the south, in the 1st Brigade's sector, Brigadier-General W. A. Griesbach, the brigade commander, rode up on his charger with mounted orderlies in attendance to direct operations. He was as cool as though on manoeuvres, and when his horse was wounded he merely transferred to another.

By nightfall the Canadians everywhere held the line of the Canal du Nord. The 1st and 4th divisions had now advanced almost five miles through some of the best prepared defensive positions on the Western Front, but the beaten enemy had exacted a high price. In these days Canadian infantry soldiers were apt to smile grimly if they heard comments that German morale was breaking. Between September 1 and September 3, 297 Canadian officers and 5,325 other ranks had been killed or wounded.

While the troops had been fighting, senior commanders and staff were planning the next phase of the offensive. More than a week before the Canal du Nord had been reached, General Sir Julian Byng had spent a morning at Canadian Corps headquarters at Noyelle Vion talking to his friend, Lieutenant-General Sir Arthur Currie. At the conclusion of the unofficial conference Byng stood in front of the large-scale map on the wall of the Operations Room, his face serious and his eyes thoughtful. At last he nodded slowly and spoke half to himself.

"It's the best possible plan."

He was silent for a moment more, then turned abruptly from the map and looked up at the huge figure beside him.

"Old man, do you think you can do it?"

Currie's eyes were as serious as Byng's. Both knew how much was at stake and what the tragic price would be. Slowly the Canadian commander nodded, and without another word the two generals turned and left the room.

In keeping with Marshal Foch's over-all plan, the enemy was to be attacked unceasingly. The French would assault on the Aisne; the French and Americans would drive towards St. Mihiel and Mézières; the Belgians would advance towards Ghent; and the British would attack towards Cambrai and St. Quentin. Yet before Cambrai was reached the Canal du Nord had to be passed, the Marquion Line, a mile east of the canal, had to be pierced, the commanding height of Bourlon Wood had to be cleared, and finally the Marcoing Line itself had to be broken.

For much of its length the Canal du Nord was an impassable obstacle, flanked by flooded marshes and covered by hundreds of well-sited machine guns. Currie did not even consider a straightforward frontal attack. To the south, however, opposite Inchy-en-Artois, the canal had not been completed and its bed was dry. Boldly, Currie decided to pass the entire corps through this narrow defile, although his assaulting battalions would have an initial frontage of attack of only 3,000 yards. Once the canal had been crossed the corps's front would soon have to fan out to a width of 9,700 yards.

This difficult set-piece operation took time to prepare. Artillery fire plans had to be worked out, ammunition had to be dumped, and, most important of all, the enemy defences had to be studied thoroughly. All through September observation balloons floated above the Canadian lines, while in the cupolas officers studied the length of the Canal du Nord through field glasses. Whenever an enemy aeroplane appeared these balloons had to be pulled down quickly. Sometimes this could not be done in time and then the sausage-shaped hydrogen bag would explode with a great puff of flame, and the observer – if he was lucky – would parachute to the ground.

At last everything was ready. On the cold, damp evening of September 26 the assaulting battalions of the 1st and 4th divisions assembled in deepening twilight for the crossing of the Canal du Nord. One brigade of the 4th Division would attack on the right and two brigades of the 1st Division on the left. In the second phase of the operation the 11th British Division would come into line on the left of the 1st Division and the 3rd Division would take up position on the right of the 4th. Through the hours of darkness the men huddled together amid the tangled wire and debris of the old Drocourt-Quéant Line, waiting for daybreak and the barrage that would begin at 5.20. Just before first light the overcast sky cleared and the day dawned fine with only a few fluffy white clouds floating across a blue sky before a light west wind.

At zero hour the barrage descended like a long white cloud along the Canadian front. As soon as the enemy discovered he was being attacked, his guns opened up on the canal, and in spite of effective Canadian counter-battery work some shells fell among the soldiers crowded in the dry canal bed. Nevertheless, the men moved steadily forward, swarming up the eastern bank like so many ants. On the far side, the eight tanks supporting each division proved invaluable in crushing wire and silencing machine-gun nests, although the light shells they fired often bounced along the hard ground like stones skipped across water.

164

Once across the canal, the infantry made their way, in single file and at the double, through the narrow lanes in the German wire, while machine-gun bullets struck a multitude of intimidating sparks from the adjacent entanglements. Bourlon Village was quickly captured, but since the British 63rd Division to the south was unable to keep pace, a defensive right flank had to be formed. Because of this, Bourlon Wood, the key to the defence of the area, could not be surrounded from the south and the troops in Bourlon Village were left in an exposed salient where they suffered heavy casualties. On the left flank, a portion of the Marquion Line was cleared, and, although the leading troops were checked for a time by fire from a railway embankment north of Bourlon, they overcame this and passed on to their final objectives.

By 12.30 the enemy was retiring all across the front in some disorder. As resistance crumbled, battalion Lewis guns, firing at long range, cut down many German infantrymen who were streaming back towards the farmhouses known as Pilgrim's Rest and La Maison Neuve. Along the Arras-Cambrai road German artillerymen could be seen trying to save their guns, and some fieldpieces were actually being hauled by long lines of men on drag ropes. Wagons, infantry, limbers, and motor lorries, all mixed together, were pressing back to Cambrai, whose spires and towers were plainly visible only some three miles away.

By two in the afternoon the intermediate objective midway between the villages of Marquion and Haynecourt had been reached, and Canadian troops had passed through to capture Haynecourt. Later in the afternoon, patrols had penetrated as far as the Douai-Cambrai road. By twilight the Canadians were probing the Marcoing Line.

Meanwhile the 3rd Brigade had crossed the canal and swung north to capture the villages of Marquion and Sains-les-Marquion, thus clearing the way for the 11th British Division to come into action. The three assaulting battalions were all firmly on their objectives by two o'clock in the afternoon. At one stage, in front of the village of Marquion, when two Canadian companies both sadly depleted by casualties were held up by German fire, a battalion of the Manchester Regiment opportunely arrived. The British attacked in fine

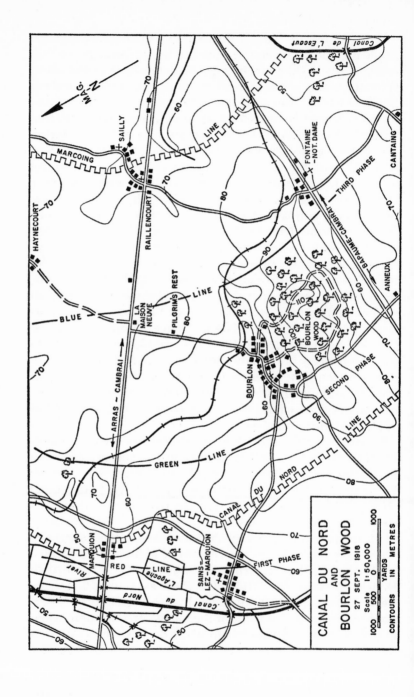

CANAL DU NORD
AND
BOURLON WOOD
27 SEPT. 1918
Scale 1:50,000

1000   500   0   1000 YARDS
1000   1000 METRES
CONTOURS IN METRES

style and, together with the Canadians, cleared Marquion and swept on.

Everywhere the day had gone well. All through the afternoon and early evening dejected files of German prisoners tramped to the rear. They were a very mixed bag; most were in the customary grey of the infantry, but there were also huge dragoons and cuirassiers in red-strapped field uniforms and uhlans, and members of one unit were clad in sombre black.

Neither the 3rd Division nor the 4th Division had gained as much ground as the 1st on September 27, but that night General Currie noted in his diary: "Today's success jeopardizes the hold of the enemy on the Drocourt-Quéant system north of the Scarpe and he may be expected to pull back to Douai." The attacks which began again on the 28th were aimed at approaching Cambrai from the north and preventing the Germans from building a defensive line west of that city.

However, the first day's success was not to be repeated, for resistance had stiffened everywhere along the front. Moreover, German aircraft now appeared over the battlefield in considerable numbers and met little opposition from Allied planes. Many Canadian casualties were caused by the strafing of low-flying Fokkers. All through September 28 the enemy launched repeated counterattacks. Many of these were pressed with great bravery and determination – some German battalions marched into battle with buglers and drummers playing martial airs in front of them – but in each case the assaults withered away in the face of deadly defensive fire.

Yet, if the German attacks met with no success, the Canadian attacks fared little better. The 3rd and 4th divisions broke into the main Marcoing Line, but in spite of the utmost gallantry neither the 1st Division nor the 11th (British) Division made much headway. On September 29 bitter fighting again resulted in negligible gains, and the day's work cost the Canadian Corps 2,089 killed and wounded. The temporary check suffered by the Canadian Corps in front of Cambrai gave little comfort to the German high command, who plainly saw the writing on the wall. On the 29th, when Hindenburg and Ludendorff met the Kaiser at Spa, they demanded that Germany seek an armistice without delay.

On the 30th, further gallant attacks broke against a stubborn defence, although the 4th Division gained a few hundred yards and Princess Patricia's Canadian Light Infantry of the 3rd Division captured the village of Tilloy. This was infantry fighting at its most demanding. Depleted battalions which would normally have been withdrawn for rest, re-equipment, and reinforcement were committed time and again, and the weary soldiers never failed to respond.

The night of September 30–October 1 was wild with wind and rain as the assaulting battalions marched to their assembly areas over slippery, muddy roads. Although the artillery supporting the Canadians fired 7,000 tons of ammunition on October 1 – two and a half times as much as the entire tonnage fired by both sides in the South African War – the advance again encountered most determined opposition. The Canadian battalions, almost all of them down to far less than half strength, fought their way forward about a mile to the east of Tilloy.

Since a pause for reorganization was now absolutely necessary, the 2nd Division relieved the 4th Division, most of the 3rd Division,* and part of the 1st Division on the night of October 1–2. In his Special Order of October 3 General Currie wrote: "In the short period of two months the Canadian Corps – to which were attached the 32nd (British) Division for the Battle of Amiens, the 4th and 51st (British) divisions for the Battle of Arras, and the 11th (British) Division for this Battle of Cambrai – has encountered and defeated decisively 47 German divisions; that is, nearly a quarter of the total German forces on the Western Front."

Elsewhere the widely separated Allied attacks were forcing the enemy back all along the front. In one of these offensives, when General Rawlinson's Fourth Army drove forward near

---

* The 3rd Division was now commanded by Major-General F. O. W. Loomis, who replaced Major-General Lipsett on October 1. General Lipsett, a British officer, assumed command of the 4th British Division, but within two weeks he was killed while making a reconnaissance in a forward area. The entire corps mourned Lipsett's death, for he was a gallant and intelligent officer who had served with the Canadians since the beginning of the war.

Le Cateau on October 9, the Canadian Cavalry Brigade advanced eight miles and took more than 400 prisoners. That same day in the Arras sector, when the 2nd Canadian Division attacked at dawn to secure crossings over the Canal de l'Escaut, it found the Germans withdrawing on a broad front. That morning, when Canadian troops entered Cambrai, they discovered that the retreating Germans had attempted to set fire to the deserted city.

Between August 26 and October 10 the Canadian Corps had advanced twenty-three miles against the bitterest opposition and had captured 18,585 prisoners, 371 guns, and more than 2,000 machine guns. As well as capturing Cambrai, the Canadians had liberated fifty-four towns or villages. To achieve these results the Canadians had lost 1,544 officers and 29,262 other ranks.

By now the German and Austrian governments had sent notes to President Wilson of the United States asking for an immediate armistice. Germany's ally Bulgaria had already been knocked out of the war; General Allenby was pursuing a defeated Turkish army towards Aleppo; and even on the Italian front the Central Powers were menaced by superior and rejuvenated forces. None of this would have been decisive, were it not that the German army on the Western Front was on the verge of utter defeat. Its dwindling reserves could no longer be shuttled back and forth to block the hammer-blows that were falling, now here, now there, upon its crumbling line. Within the next month the mighty German army, which had marched so arrogantly into neutral Belgium in 1914 and had fought so magnificently since that time, was to be pressed and harried until it was incapable of any serious resistance.

After the fall of Cambrai the character of the war changed. Some hard fighting still lay ahead, but the Allies were now pursuing a thoroughly beaten enemy. As it turned out, the Canadians proved to be instinctively good at a war of movement, where individual initiative and resourcefulness counted for much.

By mid October autumn had descended on Europe. It was a time of dark, rainy nights and chill, clear days. In the early morning, hoar frost glistened on the grass and hedgerows and at night the soldiers were glad of an extra blanket. Now the Canadians were advancing into territory untouched by war. Instead of barbed wire, trench lines, and shell-torn ground, they passed through stubble fields, small pastures, copses with all their trees still standing, and trim, picturesque little villages. As they entered Belgium on their way to Mons, the landscape changed again and they found themselves in the midst of mining villages, slag heaps, grimy black factories with tall chimneys, and isolated farms.

The certainty of defeat did not prevent the retiring enemy from leaving booby traps behind him. The Canadians soon learned that it was dangerous to straighten a crooked picture in an empty house, to open a closed door or close an open one, to pick up an attractive souvenir left on a table or by the roadside. By now the Germans were surrendering more easily, although some units – and especially the machine-gunners – still fought as courageously as ever. Several Canadian battalions had bitter experiences with enemy officers and soldiers who came forward apparently to surrender but then opened fire and killed some of their captors. As a result, a few Canadian units lost much of their inclination to take prisoners. One battalion was almost apologetic when reporting the number of prisoners captured, stating that "it was impossible to avoid taking so many as they surrendered in batches of from 20 to 50". Even when prisoners had passed through the hazards of the forward zone they were not always safe, for as the war hastened to a close German airmen repeatedly machine-gunned the long columns of their own men who were marching back to the Canadian cages.

The enemy fought to hold Valenciennes, but on November 3 he was driven from this last halting place. On this same day Austria-Hungary signed an armistice. The war, which had begun so confidently under high midsummer suns, was now spluttering out beneath grey November skies, and the world would find the coming winter long. The Canadians advanced several miles each day and were greeted as liberators in all the towns and villages along their route. The burgomasters, the curés, old men, women, and children flocked about the troops and pressed wine, food, and flowers upon them. Often, as the khaki columns swung by, the French and Belgian civilians crowding the streets wept openly. And more often than not they could not themselves have told how much of this was due to sorrow and how much to happiness. Frequently the roads were jammed with evacuees, trudging along on foot with bundles on their backs, pushing go-carts, or driving a single horse, donkey, or ox. Sometimes a dozen men would have hitched themselves to a wagon which they pulled laboriously along. Almost all these evacuees had somewhere about them a brave little scrap of tricolour and most carts flew a flag.

When the Canadians liberated the village of Famars late one November night some of the inhabitants declined to be evacuated until the next morning, although enemy shells were falling all about the place. In the morning Canadian troops held their breath while they watched an old, white-haired couple, dressed primly in their black Sunday best, walk shakily hand in hand down the road that led away from the front. Every few minutes salvoes of German high explosive crashed down across the road but the elderly pair proceeded unharmed.

On November 10 the Canadians were in the vicinity of Mons where British troops had first been committed to action – so very long ago it seemed now – in 1914. Early on the 11th, the 42nd Battalion (Royal Highlanders of Canada) and the Royal Canadian Regiment reached the centre of the city. At 6.30 that morning Canadian Corps headquarters was advised that hostilities would cease at eleven o'clock, and by nine o'clock all front line troops had been warned. The men took the momentous news quietly. As eleven o'clock approached, the forward companies of the 31st (Alberta) Battalion saw a German officer stand up a few hundred yards away from the Canadian outposts. The German fired a white Very light in the air, then his men rose from the ground around him and began calmly to dismantle their machine guns, pouring the water out of their jackets. When they had packed up their equipment, like men who put away their tools at the end of a day's work, they fell in, turned into column, and marched off to the east along the road to Boissoit. That night the Germans put on a boisterous fireworks display, firing off every flare they could find.

171

In December and January the 1st and 2nd divisions served with the Allied Army of Occupation on the right bank of the Rhine but then rejoined the 3rd and 4th divisions in Belgium where the corps did garrison duty until it could be returned to Canada. At Currie's insistence, most of the Canadian Expeditionary Force came home as formed units to be demobilized in the centres where they had been raised. By the end of September 1919 the great majority of Canadian soldiers had become civilians again.

The survivors of the First Contingent especially found the country to which they returned different in many ways from the one they had left. The years between 1914 and 1919 formed a dark abyss that cut across the continuity of the past. The war had changed forever the course of history, although in ways which none of the belligerents had foreseen or desired. Nearly 620,000 Canadians had joined the army out of a population of only 8,000,000. A total of 61,326 Canadians had been killed and 172,950 wounded. The war brought in its wake constitutional changes that entirely altered Canada's position in relation to Britain and the rest of the world and that spelled the end of the British Empire as it had been in 1914. Great industrial changes had been effected, as Canada diversified her manufactured products, produced many items that had formerly been imported, and more than quadrupled her export trade. Great social changes had taken place, as women went to work in the factories, urban populations swelled, and labour organized on an unprecedented scale. Government expenditures had increased from about $130 million annually to almost $3,000 million in four years, and most of this huge sum was war debt, left for future generations to pay. After 1918 the interest on Canada's war debt was almost $150 million a year – more than the total government expenditure of pre-war years. In these and other particulars the war was decisive, even if the results were in the main the opposite of the Canadian war aims and not in the least what had been intended.

In another sense, of course, the war had not been decisive at all. The German army, it is true, had been thoroughly beaten in the field – the subsequent legend that it had returned home undefeated only to be "stabbed in the back" at the Peace

Conference was a downright lie – but the victorious Allies were soon to see Germany grow strong again. And it was to be a new Germany, embittered by defeat, frustrated by the imposed terms of peace, vengeful and determined to reverse the verdict of 1918. Thus did an unnecessary war lead to a necessary one.

Indeed, it is already becoming apparent that the two world wars of the twentieth century were really one war – a German war in two phases, separated by a long armistice. It would appear, too, that the first phase – the First World War – was historically the more important. The real revolutions came as a result of the first German war. Europe ceased to be the centre of the world; new forms of government emerged; the state everywhere assumed, and retained, additional powers and in some instances became absolute. Communism stepped forward out of the shadows and monarchy retreated towards them. Society's goals, aspirations, and ideals underwent significant changes, and the very light by which men looked at the world was not to seem the same again.

Since this is so, it is a pity that a whole generation of Canadians is growing up in almost complete ignorance of the events that did so much to shape their world. The study of military history, even of Canadian military history, has been much neglected in Canada, for too many Canadian historians look askance at it, regarding it as a subject too brutal and barbarian for the groves of their Academy. They can debate learnedly on the social, economic, religious, geographical, and political factors that have influenced Canadian development, but all too many of them ignore or undervalue the military factor. Yet war and military considerations have frequently been paramount, and have always been important, themes in Canadian history.

This relative neglect is in large part a reaction against the seeming futility of twentieth-century war, but futilities are not dissipated by ignoring them. There is, moreover, another side to the coin. In unprecedented measure the First World War brought forth heroism, sacrifice, comradeship, and devotion, as well as much agony, sorrow, selfishness, and stupidity. At the end, certainly, there was no brave new world, or even any permanent peace, but the Canadian soldiers who returned home, and their dead comrades who remained in France and Flanders, had done their duty well. The failure was not theirs.

The Canadian Corps in France

As of November 1918 the Canadian Corps in France, with a strength of 156,441 all ranks, consisted of the following major formations and units:

Canadian Corps Headquarters

Cavalry	3	regiments
	1	squadron
Artillery	4	field brigades
	1	anti-aircraft battery
	3	brigades garrison artillery
Engineers	5	army troops companies
	1	searchlight company
	1	tunnelling company
	1	survey section
	2	tramways companies
Machine-gun Corps	2	motor machine-gun brigades
Army Service Corps	7	motor transport companies
Medical Corps	8	general hospitals
	6	stationary hospitals
	4	casualty clearing stations
	2	field ambulance units
Railway Troops	13	battalions
	1	railway construction unit
Labour	4	infantry workshops companies
	5	area employment companies

Each of the four infantry divisions consisted of the following major units:

Artillery	2	brigades field artillery, each of three field batteries and one howitzer battery

| *Infantry* | 3 | brigades, each of four infantry battalions and a trench mortar battery. Each Canadian infantry battalion had a strength of approximately 1,000 men and a Canadian division had a total strength of approximately 21,000. |

In addition, each division had on its establishment one machine-gun battalion, one divisional train Canadian Army Service Corps, three field ambulances, and one employment company.

Sources

Apart from unit and formation war diaries and other official records held by the Public Archives of Canada and the Directorate of History, Canadian Forces Headquarters, the following are among the works consulted:

The Adjutant. *The 116th Battalion in France*. Toronto, 1921.

Bennett, Captain S. G. *The 4th Canadian Mounted Rifles*. Toronto, 1926.

Biggs, Reverend E. R. *Historical Record of the 76th Overseas Battalion of the Canadian Expeditionary Force*. Toronto, n.d.

Buchan, John. *A History of the Great War*. 4 vols. London, 1922.

Canada in the Great World War. 6 vols. Toronto, 1917-21.

Canadian War Records. Compiled by the Historical Section of the General Staff. Ottawa, 1920.

Churchill, Winston S. *The World Crisis 1911-1918*. 4 vols. London, 1949.

Cornloup, Claudius. *L'Epopée du Vingt-Deuxième*. Montreal, 1919.

Corrigall, Major D. J. *The History of the 20th Canadian Battalion (Central Ontario Regiment)*. Toronto, 1935.

Duguid, Colonel A. Fortescue. *History of the Canadian Forces 1914-19*. (Canadian official history.) Ottawa, 1938.

Edmonds, Brigadier-General Sir James E. *History of the Great War: Military Operations France and Belgium*. 23 vols. (British official history.) London, 1922-47.

Falls, Cyril. *The Great War 1914-1918*. New York, 1955.

Fetherstonhaugh, R. C. *The 24th Battalion C.E.F.: Victoria Rifles of Canada*. Montreal, 1930.

————— *The 13th Battalion Royal Highlanders of Canada.* Montreal, 1925.

————— *The Royal Montreal Regiment, 14th Battalion C.E.F.* Montreal, 1927.

Gardner, R. B. *The Big Push.* London, 1961.

German Official History. *Der Weltkrieg 1914 bis 1918.* 14 vols. Berlin, 1925-57.

Gibbs, Philip. *The Battles of the Somme.* London, 1917.

Goodspeed, Lieutenant-Colonel D. J. *Battle Royal: A History of the Royal Regiment of Canada, 1862-1962.* Toronto, 1962.

————— *Ludendorff: Genius of World War I.* Toronto, 1966.

————— (ed.). *The Armed Forces of Canada, 1867-1967.* Ottawa, 1967.

Haig, Field Marshal Sir Douglas. *Sir Douglas Haig's Despatches,* ed. J. H. Boraston. London, 1920.

————— *The Private Papers of Douglas Haig,* ed. Robert Blake. London, 1952.

Hart, Liddell. *A History of the World War, 1914-1918.* London, 1930.

Hayes, Lieutenant-Colonel Joseph. *The Eighty-Fifth in France and Flanders.* Halifax, 1920.

Hodder-Williams, Ralph. *Princess Patricia's Canadian Light Infantry.* 2 vols. Toronto, 1923.

Johnston, Lieutenant-Colonel G. Chambers. *The 2nd Canadian Mounted Rifles (British Columbia Horse).* Vernon, B.C., n.d.

McEvoy, Bernard, and Captain A. H. Finlay. *History of the 72nd Canadian Infantry Battalion Seaforth Highlanders of Canada.* Vancouver, 1920.

Michel, Jacques. *La Participation des Canadiens Français à la Grande Guerre.* Montreal, n.d.

Murray, Colonel W. W. *The History of the 2nd Canadian Battalion (East. Ontario Regiment).* Ottawa, 1947.

Nicholson, Colonel G. W. L. *Canadian Expeditionary Force 1914-1919.* (Canadian official history.) Ottawa, 1962.

————— *The Fighting Newfoundlander.* Newfoundland, 1964.

————— *The Gunners of Canada,* vol. I. Toronto, 1967.

Report of the Ministry, Overseas Military Forces of Canada, 1918. London, n.d.

Russenholt, E. S. *Six Thousand Canadian Men: Being the History of the 44th Battalion Canadian Infantry, 1914-1919.* Winnipeg, 1932.

Scott, Canon F. G. *The Great War as I Saw It.* Toronto, 1922.

Scudamore, Major T. V. *A Short History of the 7th Battalion, C.E.F.* Vancouver, 1930.

Singer, H. C., and A. A. Peebles. *History of the 31st Battalion, C.E.F.* Calgary, 1939.

Steele, Captain Harwood. *The Canadians in France, 1915-1918.* Toronto, 1920.

Swettenham, Captain John A. *To Seize the Victory: The Canadian Corps in World War I.* Toronto, 1965.

Terraine, John. *Douglas Haig: The Educated Soldier.* London, 1963.

———— *The Western Front 1914-1918.* London, 1964.

Topp, Lieutenant-Colonel C. Beresford. *The 42nd Battalion C.E.F.: Royal Highlanders of Canada.* Montreal, 1931.

Urquhart, Lieutenant-Colonel H. M. *The History of the 16th Battalion (The Canadian Scottish).* Toronto, 1932.

Watt, Richard M. *Dare Call It Treason.* New York, 1963.

Wood, Lieutenant-Colonel H. F. *Vimy!* Toronto, 1967.

Index

Aisne River, 16, 162, 163
Aitken, Sir Max, 131
Aix Noulette, 98
Albatross (aircraft), 85
Albert, 64, 65, 70, 155
Albrecht of Württemberg, Duke, 31
Alderson, Lieutenant-General E. A. H., 11, 21, 39, 40, 43, 46, 54, 58, 114
"Alderson's Force", 43, 45
Aleppo, 169
Allenby, General Sir E., 81, 121, 169
Allied Army of Occupation, 172
Allison, Hon. Colonel J. W., 126
American Ammunition Company, 126
Amiens, Battle of, 140-53, 155, 156, 168
Ancre River, 141
Argonne, the, 155
Arleux Loop, 94
Armagh Wood, 59, 60
Arras, 27, 70, 81, 155
Artois, 81, 82, 96
Asquith, H. H., 5, 6
Aubers Ridge, 40
Avre River, 141, 143

Bapaume, 65, 155
Bazentin Ridge, 69
Beaucourt Wood (Amiens), 149
Beaumont Hamel, 65

Bellevue Spur (Passchendaele), 117
Below, General von, 82
Bennett, R. B., 129
Berlin, 8
Bethmann-Holweg, Chancellor, 80
Béthune, 48, 107
Black Hand Society, 2
Bois de la Folie, 89
Bois de l'Hirondelle, 96
Bois Hugo, 99, 105
Bois Rasé, 98
Bois du Vert, 157
Borden, Sir Robert, 4, 5, 6, 7, 9, 54, 127-34, 136-7
Bouchoir, 150
Bourassa, Henri, 135
Bourlon Wood, 162, 163, 165
Brest-Litovsk, 122
Brickfields, the, 70
British Expeditionary Force, 17
Brown, Private Harry, V.C., 103-4
Bruchési, Archbishop, 132
Brutinel, Brigadier-General R., 142, 159
Buissy Switch, 160
Bully Grenay, 102
Burstall, Major-General H. E., 50, 99, 140, 157
Byng, General Sir Julian, 58, 65, 84, 85, 91, 121, 155, 163

Cabinet War Committee (British), 112
Cagnicourt, 160, 162
Cailleux, Madame, 3
Caix, 142
Cambrai, 156, 163, 169
Cambrai, Battle of, 121
Canadian Cavalry Brigade, 169
Canadian Expeditionary Force, 10, 11, 17
Canadian Light Horse, The, 90, 91
"Canadian Orchard", 41, 43-6
Canal de l'Escaut, 169
Canal du Nord, 156, 157, 160, 162-5
Candy Trench, 73
Cape Hellas, 55
Caporetto, Battle of, 115
Cavan, General Lord, 76
Chantilly, 65
Chapel Hill, 155, 157
Charteris, Brigadier-General J., 123
Chaulnes, 147
Chemin des Dames, 139
Chicory Trench, 100, 102, 104
Churchill, Winston, 5-6, 69, 72, 112
Cinnabar Trench (Hill 70), 106
Cité St. Auguste, 100, 102
Cité St. Edouard, 99
Cité Ste. Elisabeth, 96, 99, 100
Cité St. Emile, 96, 100
Cité St. Laurent, 96, 99
Combat Trench (Hill 70), 106
Commandant's House, 83
Commotion Trench, 100
Compiègne, 155
Contalmaison, 65, 71
Contingent, First Canadian, 8, 12, 14; Second Canadian, 14
Coronel, Battle of, 9
Courcelette, 73, 74
Crest Farm (Passchendaele), 119
Crow's Nest, the, 159
Currie, Lieutenant-General Sir Arthur, 21, 33, 37, 44-5, 54, 70, 82, 88, 91, 96, 97, 100, 102, 106, 108, 113-14, 119, 120, 134, 140, 151, 152, 156, 157, 159, 160, 163, 167, 168, 172

Dardanelles, the, 55, 58
Davis, Hon. Capt. W. H., 118
Debeney, General Eugène, 141
Decline Copse (Passchendaele), 117
Delville Wood, 65
Demuin, 145
Desire Trench, 77
Domart, 148
Douai Plain, 81, 97
Drocourt-Quéant Line, 156, 160, 162, 164, 167
Drury, 162
Dual Entente, 2, 4, 5
Duck Lodge (Passchendaele), 119
"Duck's Bill", the, 49, 50

Edward, J. W., 132
Essars, 48

Fabeck Graben, 70
Falkenhausen, General von, 82, 87, 91
Falkenhayn, General von, 20, 56, 70, 71, 138
Famars, 171
Farbus Wood, 83, 88, 90
Fayolle, General, 68
Festubert, 40-8, 52, 63, 79, 83, 114
Fiset, Major-General Sir Eugène, 128
Fisher, Corporal Frederick, 24
Flavelle, Joseph, 125
Foch, Marshal Ferdinand, 27, 29, 30, 112, 139, 140, 155, 163
Fokker (aircraft), 71, 167
Fortuin, 110
Fosse St. Louis (Hill 70), 107
Fouquescourt, 151
Franz Ferdinand, Archduke, 3
French, Field Marshal Sir John, 27, 38, 53, 54-5
Fresnes-Rouvroy Line, 155, 157, 158, 159
Fresnoy, 95
Frezenberg Ridge, 34

Gault, Captain A. Hamilton, 10, 11
Gentelles Wood, 143
George V, King, 81n., 92
Ghent, 163

Ginley, Anthony, 42
Givenchy, 48, 49, 52, 53, 83
Good Hope, H.M.S., 9
Gotha (aircraft), 111, 159
Goudberg, 120
Gough, General Sir Henry, 73, 113, 114, 139
Gravenstafel Ridge, 21, 33
Green Crassier, the, 107
Grey, Sir Edward, 4, 5
Griesbach, Brigadier-General W. A., 162
Guémappe, 157
Guillaucourt, 145, 147
Guise, 16
Gwatkin, Major-General W. G., 128

Hague Conventions, 20
Haig, Field Marshal Sir Douglas, 17; at Festubert, 39-40; 45, 46, 48, 53, 55, 58, 61, 63, 64, 65, 66; on Australian generals, 69, 72, 77; promoted field marshal, 81n.; 94, 95, 97, 108, 111, 112, 114, 120, 121-3, 139, 151
Halifax, 10
Hamon Wood (Amiens), 145
Hangard, 148
Hangard Wood (Amiens), 145
"Hanging Virgin" of Albert, 70
Hazebrouck, 17
Hendecourt, 159
Hessian Trench, 74
High Seas Fleet, 5
Hill 61, 59
Hill 70, 59, 96-108
Hill 145 (Vimy), 88, 89, 91
Hill Top Ridge, 27, 28, 29, 30, 33
Hindenburg, Field Marshal Paul von, 70, 71, 167
Hindenburg Line, 77, 81, 121, 155, 162
Hoffmann, Major-General Max, 56
Hooge, 56
Horne, General Sir H. S., 81, 97, 108
Hughes, Major-General Sam, 4, 6, 8, 10, 11, 12, 32, 48, 53, 54, 126-7, 134n., 136
Hugo Trench (Hill 70), 105

Hull, Brigadier-General C. P. A., 33
Humbert, General, 155

Imperial Munitions Board, 125
Inchy-en-Artois, 163
"Indian Village", 42
Infantry battalions, Canadian:
    Princess Patricia's Canadian Light Infantry, 11, 34, 56, 60, 119, 168
    Royal Canadian Regiment, The, 56, 171
    1st (Ontario) Battalion, 27-8, 50, 51, 61, 120
    2nd (East. Ontario) Battalion, 27-8, 52, 61, 105, 120
    3rd Battalion (The Toronto Regiment), 28, 33, 45-6, 51, 52, 61, 120
    4th Battalion, 27-8, 61
    5th Battalion, 33, 45, 60, 103
    7th (British Columbia) Battalion, 28, 33, 61, 100, 101, 121
    8th (Winnipeg) Battalion, 31-3, 61, 100, 101, 121
    10th Battalion, 24, 26, 33, 103
    13th Battalion (Royal Highlanders of Canada), 61, 62, 70, 100
    14th Battalion (Royal Montreal Regiment), 28, 33, 41, 42, 43, 160
    15th Battalion (48th Highlanders of Canada), 28, 31-3, 100
    16th (Canadian Scottish) Battalion, 25, 26, 41-4, 61, 62, 76, 99, 100
    18th (Western Ontario) Battalion, 58
    20th (Central Ontario) Battalion, 58, 100, 104-5, 121
    21st (Eastern Ontario) Battalion, 58, 89
    22nd (French Canadian) Battalion, 73
    24th Battalion (Victoria Rifles), 100
    25th Battalion (Nova Scotia Rifles), 73, 89

26th (New Brunswick) Battalion, 100

27th (City of Winnipeg) Battalion, 57, 90, 120

28th (North West) Battalion, 61, 120

29th (Vancouver) Battalion, 57, 90, 106-7

31st (Alberta) Battalion, 57, 89, 120, 154, 171

42nd Battalion (Royal Highlanders of Canada), 147, 171

44th Battalion, 107, 117

46th Battalion, 107, 117

47th Battalion, 107

49th (Edmonton) Battalion, 60

50th Battalion, 107

52nd (Lake Superior) Battalion, 61, 118

58th Battalion, 61, 62, 117

72nd Battalion (Seaforth Highlanders of Canada), 119

78th Battalion (Winnipeg Grenadiers), 119

85th Battalion (Nova Scotia Highlanders), 119

116th Battalion, 98

1st Canadian Mounted Rifles, 59

4th Canadian Mounted Rifles, 59, 60, 117, 118

5th Canadian Mounted Rifles, 119

Island Traverse, 83

Isonzo, Battles of the, 80

Janney, Captain E. L., 10

Jellicoe, Admiral Sir John, 112

Jerusalem, capture of, 122

Joffre, General, 65, 77, 81

Kenora Trench, 74

Ketchen, Brigadier-General H. D. B., 57, 58

Kiggell, Lieutenant-General Sir Launcelot, 111, 123

Kitchener, Lord, 10, 11, 67

Kitchener's Wood, 25, 26, 27, 33, 34, 37

Kluck, General von, 16

La Bassée Canal, 40, 49

La Folie Farm, 83

Lansdowne, Lord, 80

La Quinque Rue, 41

Laurier, Sir Wilfrid, 7, 12, 132-3, 137

Learmonth, Major O. M., V.C., 105

Le Cateau, 16, 169

Lee-Enfield rifle, 49

Lens, 81, 96, 97, 98, 99, 106, 107

Lens-Béthune road, 98, 102

Le Quesnel, 142, 147, 150

Les Tilleuls, 89

Liège, 8

Lipsett, Major-General L. J., 61, 73, 88, 140, 157, 158; death, 168n.

Lloyd George, David, 39, 69, 72, 112, 122-3, 130, 137

Locality "C", 21, 37

Long, Walter, 129

Loomis, Major-General F. O. W., 21, 168n.

Loos, 98, 102, 104

Lord Strathcona's Horse, 46, 149

Lossberg, Colonel Fritz von, 37, 82, 115, 155

Louvain, 8

Luce River, 145-6, 148

Ludendorff, General Erich, 37, 70, 71, 77, 92, 94, 106, 136, 138, 139, 140, 151, 153, 155, 168

Macdonell, Major-General Sir A. C., 99, 140

McGillivray, Piper Alex, 99-100

McNaughton, General A. G. L., 114n.

Manchester Regiment, The, 165

Mangin, General Charles, 155

Marcoing Line, 156, 163, 167

Marqueffles Farm, 98

Marquion Line, 156

Marwitz, General von der, 141

Marzingarbe, 98, 104

Masurian Lakes, 16

Mauser Ridge, 27, 28, 29, 30

Meetcheele, 119

Méharicourt, 150

Meighen, Arthur, 133

Menin Gate, 109, 111

Menin Road, 56
Mercer, Major-General M. S., 45-6, 56, 59
Mewburn, General S. C., 134
Mézières, 163
Military Service Act, 132, 135, 136
Military Voters' Act, 133
Millerand, E. A., 54
Moltke, General Helmuth von, 16, 48
Monchy-le-Preux, 155
Mons, 171
Montauban, 68
Moreuil Wood (Amiens), 147
Morrison, Brigadier-General E. W. B., 84, 115
Mosselmarkt, 120
Mount Kemmel, 141
Mount Sorrel, 59, 60, 62
Mouquet Farm, 65, 70, 74
Mouse Trap Farm, 25, 29, 30, 33
Mutiny of French Army, 95-6

Nabob Alley, 100
Neuve Chapelle, 40
Neuville St. Vaast, 85
Neuville-Vitasse, 154-5
Newfoundland Regiment, The, 55; at Beaumont Hamel, 68
Nieuport (aircraft), 71
Nine Elms, 83
Niobe, H.M.C.S., 9
Nivelle, General Robert, 81, 94, 95, 112
Norman Trench (Hill 70), 100, 103
Nun's Alley, 100, 106

Oblinghem, 48
Observatory Ridge, 59, 60, 62
Ocean Work, 159
Orange Hill, 140-1, 155, 157
O'Rourke, Private Michael, V.C., 101
Ostend, 96, 112, 113

Parvillers, 151
Passchendaele, Battle of, 36, 79, 109-23, 134, 138, 140, 160
Perley, Sir George, 130, 134
Pétain, General Henri Philippe, 95, 122
Petawawa, Camp, 4

Petrograd, 84
Picardy, 148
Pimple, the, 83, 88, 91
Ploegsteert, 53
Plumer, General Sir H. C. O., 21, 58, 115
Plymouth Sound, 13
Poincaré, President Raymond, 122
Potijze, 109
Pozières, 65, 69, 70, 74
Princip, Gabriel, 2, 5

Rainbow, H.M.C.S., 9
Ravesbeek, 117
Rawlinson, General Sir Henry, 17, 67, 73, 113, 141, 151, 168
Regina Trench, 74, 76
Reims, 95
Rennie, Lieutenant-Colonel R., 45
Richardson, Piper James, V.C., 76
Richthofen, Baron von, 85
Rifle Wood (Amiens), 145
Robertson, Field Marshal Sir William, 96
Ross rifle, 32, 49
Rouvroy, 150
Royal Canadian Dragoons, 46, 52, 149
Royal Canadian Navy, 9, 10
Royal Flying Corps, 10, 82, 85, 118
Royal Naval Air Service, 9, 10
Royal Navy, 5, 9
Rupprecht of Bavaria, Crown Prince, 91

St. Eloi, 56-9, 62
St. Jean, 110
St. Julien, 24, 25, 31, 32, 33, 49, 110
St. Mihiel, 163
St. Nazaire, 14
St. Omer, 64
St. Quentin, 163
Salisbury Plain, 13
Salonika, 55
Sanctuary Wood, 59, 62
Sarajevo, 2, 3, 5
Sausage Valley, 70
Scarpe River, 155, 156, 157, 162, 167
Schlieffen, General Graf von, 16

Schlieffen Plan, 14, 16, 56
Scott, Canon F. G., 25
Seely, Brigadier-General the Rt. Hon. J. E. B., 46
"Seely's Detachment", 46
Sensée River, 158
Sharpe, Lieutenant W. F. N., 10
Shell Committee, 126
Smith-Dorrien, General Sir Horace, 21, 34
Snipe Hall (Passchendaele), 119
Soissons, 70, 155
Somme, Battle of the, 52, 61, 63, 64-79, 81, 82, 83, 113, 114, 121, 142
Source Farm (Passchendaele), 119
South African War, 4, 8, 126, 168
Spad (aircraft), 71
Stuff Redoubt, 74
Sugar Factory, the, 65, 73
Sulva Bay, 55

Tait, Sir Thomas, 129
Tannenberg, 16
Tara Hill, 77
Terraine, John, 45, 72
Thélus Village, 83, 88, 89
Thiepval, 65, 74
Tilloy, 168
Tor Top, 59, 60, 61, 62
Townshend, General Sir Charles, 55
Turko-Graben, 89
Turner, Lieutenant-General Sir R. E. W., 21, 29, 33, 37, 41, 54, 58, 73
Tuxford, Brigadier-General G. S., 61

Upton Wood, 159

Valcartier, 11, 12
Valenciennes, 170
Vapour Farm (Passchendaele), 119
Verdun, Battle of, 56, 65, 71, 80, 81, 138
Vienna Cottage (Passchendaele), 119
Villers-Bretonneux, 143, 147, 151
Vimy Ridge, 40, 50, 77, 82-93, 108
Vine Cottage (Passchendaele), 120
Vis-en-Artois Switch, 155, 158, 159
Vlamertinghe, 19, 20, 31
Von Loën Weg, 83

War Office, British, 4n.
War-Times Election Act, 133
Watson, Major-General David, 63, 77, 88, 140
Wellington, Duke of, 52
White, Sir Thomas, 126
Wieltje, 30, 110
Wiencourt, 145, 147
Wilhelm II, Kaiser, 2, 80, 153, 168
Willerval, 90, 91
Williams, Brigadier-General V. A. S., 59
Wilson, Woodrow, 80, 169
Wolfe Copse (Passchendaele), 118
Woodland Plantation (Passchendaele), 119

Ypres, 19, 49, 59, 109
Ypres, First Battle of, 17
Ypres, Second Battle of, 18-38, 40, 43, 83
Ypres, Third Battle of. See Passchendaele
Ypres Salient, 17, 18-38, 56, 58, 65, 96, 110, 112, 121, 142, 146
Yser Canal, 24, 27, 28, 31, 109

Zeebrugge, 96, 112
Zillebeke Lake, 59
Zivy Tunnel, 86
Zollern Graben, 74
Zwischen Stellung, 83